# Of Faith and Freedom

# OF FAITH AND FREEDOM

How Americans of faith can heal an ailing nation

JOE GILBERT

ISBN-10: 1523713909
ISBN-13: 9781523713905
Library of Congress Control Number: 2016931042
CreateSpace Independent Publishing Platform
North Charleston, South Carolina

# ACKNOWLEDGEMENTS

I HAVE so many people to thank for helping to make this work a reality. First, of course, my Lord and Savior Jesus Christ. As my strength and my guide, He made this all possible and granted me the perseverance and inspiration to see it through. To Kelly, my wonderful and lovely fiancé, life partner, cheerleader, and best friend who believed in me and patiently listened to my rants and raves against the system. My son Nicholas, Pastor Kirk Gilchrist for reassuring me and keeping me spiritually and doctrinally on track. A special thank you to Pastor Dan Klebes of the Indian River Baptist Church in little Philadelphia, NY, for all your advice and guidance!

I dedicate this work to my mother, Shirley Irene Gilbert. She was a saint who always saw the best in everyone. She was the shining example of stick-toitiveness, good humor and faith. She stood by and believed in me and all of her kids through thick and thin, no matter what May our good Lord keep and protect her. Heaven is now a much better place because of her presence.

# Table of Contents

# INTRODUCTION

## *THE GOOD OLD DAYS*

When you do the things that you can do, you will find a way.

—A. A. MILNE

**Galatians 5:1** It was for freedom that Christ set us free; therefore keep standing firm and do not be subject again to a yoke of slavery.

HELLO, MY FELLOW Patriot! Hey, I need your help. It seems I've lost something dear to me, and I could really use your help in finding it. It is something really important, and everyone will benefit once we find it again. I won't be able to do it without you. Given that you're already here, I'm guessing I can count on you.

It's America. I've lost it. Or, rather, we've all lost it. It was right here last I looked, but now it seems that when we turned our backs for a short time, busy with our families, jobs, and daily lives, our America slipped away. I guess we just trusted that it would always be here. We voted for and elected people we thought would take care of it for us. They promised us jobs, prosperity, and a better life for our kids. We in turn pulled the levers in the voting booths and elected them. These representatives took an oath of office to support and defend our America, but now it's gone.

We raised our kids and sent them to government-run schools, confident they would inherit the same country we've always known. We just assumed they'd grow up like we did, respecting the same principles and with the same fundamental belief-system we all used to share. We trusted the schools to teach our kids that America is a great country and how it got that way. We expected our children to be taught our shared history and the sacrifices of past generations that made us free and kept us free. It was our fondest hope to give them a life better than our own, just as our parents did for us. However, none of that happened. The America that I once knew isn't here anymore. We have to get it back.

Do you remember where we may have left it? This America wasn't always free. Patriots fought for it and paid for it with their blood throughout its history. We wrestled thirteen colonies away from a tyrannical king and founded the greatest country ever known to mankind. Then we let it slip away.

Thelen Paulk composed a passionate poem in 1986, "A Visitor from the Past." This poem describes the metaphoric vision of a midnight visitor, a colonial minuteman, who takes us on a journey from bondage to freedom and then back into bondage again. It is a warning for all freedom-loving Americans. The message of his poem is dead on:

> I had a dream the other night, I didn't understand.
> A figure walking through the mist, with flintlock in his hand.
> His clothes were torn and dirty, as he stood there by my bed
> He took off his three-cornered, and speaking low he said:
> "We fought a revolution to secure our liberty.
> We wrote the Constitution, as a shield from tyranny.
> For future generations, this legacy we gave,
> In this the land of the free, and the home of the brave.
> The freedom we secured for you, we hoped you'd always keep,
> But tyrants labored endlessly while your parents slept,

Your freedom gone, your courage lost, you're no more than a slave,
In this the land of the free, and the home of the brave.
You buy permits to travel, and permits to own a gun,
Permits to start a business, or build a place for one.
On land you believe you own, you pay a yearly rent.
Although you have no voice in how the money's spent.
Your children must attend a school that doesn't educate.
Your Christian values can't be taught, according to the state.
You read about the current news, in a regulated press.
You pay a tax you do not owe, to please the IRS."

"Your money is no longer made of Silver or of Gold.
You trade your wealth for paper, so your life can be controlled.
You pay for crimes that make our nation, turn from God in shame.
You've taken Satan's number, as you traded in your name."
You've given government control of those who do you harm,
So they can padlock churches and steal the family farm.
And keep our country deep in debt, put men of God in jail,
Harass your fellow countrymen, while corrupted courts prevail.
Your public servants don't uphold the solemn oath they've sworn.
Your daughters visit doctors, so their children won't be born.
Your leaders ship artillery, and guns to foreign shores,
And send your sons to slaughter, fighting other people's wars.
Can you regain the freedom for which we fought and died?
Or don't you have the courage, or the faith to stand with pride?
Are there no more values for which you'll fight to save?
Or do you wish your children to live in fear and be a slave?"
People of the Republic, arise and take a stand!
Defend the Constitution, the Supreme law of the land!
Preserve our Great Republic, and God-Given Right!
And pray to God to keep the torch of Freedom burning bright!"
As I awoke he vanished, in the mist from whence he came.
His words were true, we are not Free, we have ourselves to blame.

For even now as tyrants trample each God-Given Right,
We only watch and tremble, too afraid to stand and fight.
If he stands by your bedside in a dream, while you sleep,
And wonders what remains of our Rights he fought to keep,
What would be your answer, if he called out from the grave:
"Is this still the land of the free and the home of the brave?"(1)

When I was growing up—and maybe you remember this, too—America was a great country. I was in the Boy Scouts, went to church, watched *Bugs Bunny* on Saturday mornings, and went fishing or played baseball until the street-lights came on. If you're like me, we just knew our lives would be better than those of our parents. America was the strongest country on earth. That wasn't just because our military was the biggest and baddest; we also had the strongest economy, the world's best schools, and the world's best health care—by any measurable statistic, we led the way. I was blessed to have been born an American. America is still a great country. I do worry the America I grew up in and was hoping to leave to my children is gone forever, but it doesn't have to be. Together, we can fix this. If ever there was a time in our history that we need to stand together with courage and do what we know has to be done, it is right now.

Somewhere along the way, America became two countries. There were those who were proud of our country and its heritage, Founding principles, values, and—yes—our freedom and liberty were all sources of great pride. We said the Pledge of Allegiance every morning and our prayers at least every Sunday. Little did I know that there were forces at work the entire time trying to destroy it all. The "other" America consists of those who believe this country is imperialistic, oppressive, racist and evil and must be fundamentally changed.

Now, hard at work just under the surface, there is what I truly believe is the enemy of everything we stand for as a free people. This enemy has been at this for a very long time and has been so successful for so long they no longer hide their intentions. It has come out into the open in our news media, in our universities, in our elected officials, and throughout our popular culture. This enemy wants to not only crush our freedoms, history, and values today but also erase any and every memory of what this country is, what it once was, and what we could be again. I collectively call this movement the Enemy (and I'll also use "they" throughout as the generic reference for those inspired by darkness and "we" as the reference to believers). The Enemy wants to take what was once the freest, most prosperous, and most spiritual country ever in the history of mankind and "fundamentally transform" it into its utopian vision. I, for one, don't like that vision. The enemy thinks it has won and that it's all over. I am not ready to wave any white flags of surrender just yet. Again, given that you're reading this, I'm guessing that you're not either. Good! Let's get to work.

On television or online, we watch as other countries suffer coups, civil wars, or revolutions as one tyrannical despot after another comes to power. These countries were a mess before, and they will be a mess after. In the meantime, we here in America chug along, confident that it will never happen here. Is that true? Can we be confident that our country will always remain free?

What makes America any different? What has shielded us from falling into the same situation as that of these other countries?

What is this book about? That question may be answered best by first describing what this book isn't. I'll do my best to avoid mind-numbing lists of statistics and numbers. But we do have to address what we are up against. We have to talk about where we are and how we got here. We will have to compare what "is" with what "used to be" and what "should be" again in our culture and our country.

But mainly, here we look a little deeper at how and why this country was founded, and what we'll really talk about is how America is a mess because we've drifted away from our most fundamental values, convictions, and principles. Namely, God. America is losing its soul.

Believe it or not, there is a method to this work. First, we'll look at how we got here, identifying the enemies who have attacked and still are attacking freedom. We'll examine how they are going about it and where that all started. We'll also quickly discuss some current cases ripped from our TV news and papers to show that this attack, first devised more than one hundred years ago, is still not only alive and well but is going full steam ahead, faster and more determined than ever. I'll apologize up front now if I hit on a topic more than once. All of these issues intersect and many emanate from the same place, so they will often cross paths more than once.

Next, we'll look at what should be. All societies and civilizations start with the family as their basic building block, so we'll spend some time there. The next row of bricks, if you will, in the foundation of our civilization is our towns and communities. Then there are the basic rules established in our country that define the relationship between the individual citizen and our government.

We're going to hit on more than a few big topics. Many of these could be, and in some cases have been whole books in and of themselves. So I apologize in advance for my brevity in some areas. These subjects are often addressed singularly, but they all form parts of a cohesive whole. We can't discuss social unrest without addressing the family. We can't disagree with the amount of government involvement in our lives without then discussing the government's proper place and powers.

Writing this book was a daunting task. This wasn't because there wasn't enough to write about, but because there is just so *much!* There are so many daily affronts to our personal liberties and freedom that I just couldn't keep up with it all. So instead, I decided to focus on principles at work and just use a few specific examples to illustrate my points. Second, I had to pick when to start, historically speaking. I chose to start with the Frankfurt School otherwise known as the Institute for Social Research that was founded in Germany after World War I. I know and fully recognize there were plenty of other influences on the anti-Constitutional progressive and collectivist movement in America. Woodrow Wilson's administration immediately comes to mind. He, in my opinion, until 2009 anyway, was the worst president we've ever had. So, humor me in where I started and the limitations of a simple volume. If we wanted to discuss this topic in great detail, it could be thousands of pages long. I didn't want to write that and if I had, you wouldn't read it.

As a point of clarity, throughout these pages you'll see the words "Founders" and "Framers." Our Founders are our Founding Fathers who brought America its independence through the Revolution, drafted and signed the Declaration of Independence. Our Framers are those great Americans who attended the Constitutional Convention, fought for and got our great United States Constitution ratified and oversaw the birth of this great nation.

As a former intelligence officer in the Army, when I was analyzing our enemies, what they had, and what they were up to, it wasn't enough for me to just tell the commander what was going on—or worse, what had happened. I had to answer the big question: "So what?" I'll attempt to do the same here. After we talk about these various issues, we'll take a step back and ask, "So what?" In other words, now that we have painted the picture, what do we do about it? How do we stop this and turn our country around?

Last, we'll examine how to fix the mess we're in as a country. The issues we face now may seem insurmountable, but they're not. You may feel as though you're standing alone on the beach as this tsunami of insanity is crashing over you, threatening to drown you, your family and our entire civilization. But, take heart, you're not alone.

I sincerely believe that we are at an absolutely pivotal moment in the history of mankind. If America fails, the world will follow. As Ronald Reagan prophetically said, "If we lose freedom here, there is no place to escape to. This is the last stand on Earth." (2)

We simply cannot fail. The stakes are too high. There is no greater cause worthy of our time, attention and unrelenting effort than the freedom of all mankind.

After years of study, the Frankfurt School decided that the West didn't rise up in a communist revolution because our culture was too strongly rooted in such values as family, religion and God, individualism, and free-market capitalism. Marx had predicted in his book *Das Kapital* that the middle class would disappear, the rich would only become richer, and the poor would become more desperate. Those conditions would then ferment the seeds of revolution. That wasn't what was happening in the West.

The middle class was expanding as free-market capitalism and political freedom set the conditions for economic success. The professors of the Frankfurt School realized that the West would never come over to Marxism through economic changes in conditions alone. Again, they also came to the conclusion that true power came from controlling culture more than just the means of production. Therefore to bring about the revolution, they would first have to destroy our institutions of culture. As Georg Lukacs wrote as he joined the Communist party, "Who will save us from Western civilization?" (2) Of course, he meant that he and his cohorts would.

The natural enemies of Marxism are our institutions such as God, family, national identiy, our traditions and values. The father-centered, two-parent family created an environment in which traditions, values, patriotism, loyalty, and religion and spirituality were passed on from parents to their children. It was precisely those values that prohibited a Marxist revolution. They had to go. As long as strong, traditional families existed in a country, Marxism would never really catch on. The Frankfurt School, way back in the 1920s and 1930s, decided that the institutions of God, family, and traditional marriage would be their first targets. Given the historic and deep-rooted cultural norms of the West of faith, nationality, family, any new political movement strong enough to replace our civilization would have to be, in the words of Lukacs, "demonic;" it would have to "possess the religious power which is capable of filling the entire soul; a power that characterized primitive Christianity." The movement would have to be "messianic" and could only succeed when the individual citizen believes that his or her actions are determined by "not a personal destiny, but the destiny of the community in a world that has been abandoned by God.(3) The founders of the Frankfurt School knew that people wouldn't just abandon everything they held dear overnight. They would have to very deliberately infiltrate our most cherished and trusted institutions, changing the national narrative to ever so slowly transform our society into one that would accept and embrace their brand of total government control: Marxism. Lukacs called it "abolition of culture" Aufhebung der Kultur in his native German. (4)

Lukacs' buddy at the Frankfurt School, Benjamin, was right on board, writing in his work *The Arcades Project:*

"Barbarism lurks in the very concept of culture—as the concept of a fund of values which is considered independent not, indeed, of the production process in which these values originated, but of the one in which they survive. In this way they serve the apotheosis of the latter, barbaric as it may be." (5)

"Terror and civilization are inseparable," wrote Adorno and Horkheimer in The Dialectic of Enlightenment. The solution to terror was therefore simple: dismantle civilization. Marcuse expressed their goal like this: "One can rightfully speak of a cultural revolution, since the protest is directed toward the whole cultural establishment, including [the] morality of existing society." Lukacs saw "the revolutionary destruction of society as the one and only solution to the cultural contradictions of the epoch," and argued that "such a worldwide overturning of values cannot take place without the annihilation of the old values and the creation of new ones by the revolutionaries." (6)

Then Hitler came to power, and most of the professors in the Frankfurt School fled Germany. Many of them came to the United States. Once here, they embedded themselves in our universities, government, and entertainment industries. They intentionally embedded themselves into positions where they could sow their seeds of cultural destruction to the widest possible audience.

For example, Frankfurt School student Paul Lazersfeld became the director of the Office of Radio Research at Princeton University, established in 1937. Lazersfeld wasn't alone. His researchers were fellow ISR acolytes Herta Herzog, who was his wife and became the first director of research for the Voice of America and Hazel Gaudet who became a leading national political pollster. Lazersfeld's close assistant was Frankfurt School student Frank Stanton, who subsequently became the research director of the Columbia

Broadcasting System, president of CBS's news division and ultimately president of the entire network. Stanton was also the Chairman of the Board of the RAND Corporation, and a member of President Lyndon Johnson's "kitchen cabinet." (7)

Popularly known as the "Radio Project," the mission of Princeton's Office of Radio Research was to test the thesis that mass media can influence behavior. Today we would call that propaganda. That thesis was originally drafted by Frankfurt School professor Walter Benjamin with the intent of discovering how to use the new mass media of radio for social control. More precisely, it was a study to find out how to use mass media to control the citizens. While I was in the Army, we called this Psychological Operations. This fit perfectly with the plan of the cultural Marxists.

The cultural Marxists didn't just go into mass media, they also embedded themselves in literature, television, Hollywood movies and academia. They really focused on getting into our colleges and universities. Once there they knew they could imbue their viewpoints into the most open and vulnerable among us, the youth. They've been hugely successful. It has taken just a few generations, but these evil cultural insurgents have been able to erode our nation's values, heritage, culture and even faith to the point where America is barely recognizable from what it once was.

# 2

# Losing common sense and being politically correct

**"It is from within, among yourselves – from cupidity, from corruption, from disappointed ambition and inordinate thirst for power – that factions will be formed and liberty endangered. It is against such designs, whatever disguise the actors may assume, that you have especially to guard yourselves."**

— Andrew Jackson, 1837

Man has been imbued with a unique gift. That gift is the power of discrimination. No, not that kind of discrimination where a person will treat a person or a group of people differently because of their race. For the purpose of this discussion, discriminating means the simple ability to discern right from wrong, good from bad, and to anticipate the outcome of a given action based on knowledge and wisdom from past experiences and observations.

Usually, a child only has to touch a hot stove once to learn what a bad idea it would be to do that again.

We should learn throughout our lives, and that knowledge should be passed onto future generations so the same lessons don't have to be learned and relearned over and over. Being able to choose the best among competing alternatives is what has kept people safe for thousands of years.

But, the cultural Marxist has been hard at work to convince us all of that is wrong. We're told that being discriminating is bad. It is exactly this type of thinking that will destroy our civilization. In today's cultural narrative it is called Political Correctness. Political Correctness is a fatal disease to any culture. It is an eraser that wipes clean any vestiges of what gives our culture and country its identity and values.

After the terror attacks of 9/11/2001 when my mom was in her 80s, every time she was getting on an airline flight, she was just about assured to be separated out for special screening by the TSA. This is despite the fact that never, ever has an airliner been hijacked or blown up by a 83 year-old, 110lb woman with a cane, ever. Doesn't matter. Because the Left has imbued our culture with the notion that discrimination is so awful, the government had to search the most unlikely threat to demonstrate they were not discriminating. But, at the same time, the group of unaccompanied single Muslim males in their twenties and thirties who just bought their tickets with cash moments before the flight and have no luggage would not be searched so the TSA can demonstrate that they are not racially profiling.

We as intelligent human beings can see how blatantly stupid that is. We can observe an action or series of actions, events and experiences and then determine which among them are good or bad. We can analyze all past terror attacks across the world and by being discriminant, come up with a profile of a likely and unlikely candidate for a terror attack.

This would work for economic and public policy as much as it does for moral issues and every other tasks we fill our days with such as woodworking, hunting or baking bread. If a hunter were to go out into the woods with a boom box (if you can remember what those are) blaring AC/DC and dancing, he most likely won't get a deer. If a baker trying to make a loaf of bread skips the step of adding the yeast, instead of a fluffy loaf of nice bread, they'll get a big cracker. We learn. Success is a combination of hard work, experience and knowledge. These have to be judged against what has worked in the past and the goal to be accomplished.

If we were left to employ our own abilities of reason, historical perspective, analytical thinking, and critical problem-solving skills to analyze our natural environment and our current political and economic situation, we could decide for ourselves what works and what doesn't. Our environment, of course, would have to be judged against an absolute right and absolute wrong. In order to determine what is desirable, we have to have something against which we can measure. Again, using the deer hunter example, the desirable outcome would be a freezer full of meat that would feed his family over the winter. In more ethical and moral issues, we know in most instances, killing is wrong, as is stealing. We only know that by comparing it to some absolute right. Terrorists killing innocent people, especially helpless women and children is wrong. It is even evil. We can know those acts are evil by comparing them to "good." There is a natural good and evil.

Where does that absolute right and wrong, good and evil come from? Quite simply, God. It is from the scriptures, namely the Ten Commandments, and the teachings of Jesus Christ that we have an absolute good and evil by which we should judge our actions. We get into this in much more detail later.

The modern liberal, spawned by generations of cultural Marxist propaganda, suspends all rational thought. For example, if someone were to go into the maternity ward of a hospital and start killing babies, they'd be called an evil monster, and rightfully so. However the murder of millions of unborn babies is justified, legal and called "reproductive rights" or "women's rights." Judged against an absolute right and wrong, good and evil, it would be easy to see that both of these actions are wrong, reprehensible and evil.

Nowhere else should these abilities of critical thinking come into play than in our determining the best way to govern ourselves. Mankind has been wrestling with the ultimate questions of how to best govern himself and what the best forms of government and economic systems are for eons. We can look at the French Revolution or Russia's Communist Revolution and compare those situations with our own, judging them against a desirable outcome. We can determine even what that desired outcome would be as we observe what is in our society and then evaluate it against the desired results.

Left to our own devices, we can look at Soviet or North Korean communism, comparing that to the state of liberty as an alternative—a nation that respects private property rights, setting the conditions for a more universal state of prosperity than any communist revolution has ever produced. Using comparison and contrast and cause and effect, I'm confident that any reasonable person would determine that we don't want communism here. As the Bible says in Ecclesiastes 1:9, "what has been will be again, what has been done will be done again; there is nothing new under the sun" is appropriate. There is an old joke about Soviet communism:

> After years and years of scrimping and saving, a guy in Moscow finally saved up enough money to buy a car for his family. He struts into the government-run dealership all proud of himself and ready to drive his new car home and surprise his wife.
>
> The shopper says to the dealer, "Ok, I've been dreaming about this for years, and I know exactly the car I want."
> Dealer: "Terrific! What can I get for you?"
> Citizen: "I want a four-door, five-speed sedan with a bright red paint job."
> Dealer: "Well, we can only get two-door cars with four cylinders, no five speeds."
> Citizen: "What? What do you mean?"
> Dealer: "It's the bureau. They tell the factories what cars to make and what cars we can order. My hands are tied."
> Citizen: "Wow, but ok ... I still want it with the bright red paint job."
> Dealer: "No, sorry. All our cars come in one color—black."
> Citizen: "Really? Why?"

> Dealer: "It's the government bureau. They tell the factories what color of paint to use on all the cars, and they tell us what color of cars we can sell."
> Citizen: "Damn. Ok, I'll take the black, two-door, four-cylinder car even though it isn't at all what I wanted. Where is it? I want to drive it home and surprise my wife and kids."
> Dealer: "No, sorry. None of the cars are actually here. I have to order it, but I'll need your money today."
> Citizen: "Really? This is ridiculous. How long will it take to get here?"
> Dealer: "Four years."
> Citizen: "*Four years*? That's an outrage! I have to wait *four years* for my car?"
> Dealer: "It's the bureau. They can't get anything right, and we're back ordered for the next four years."
> Citizen: "Ok, ok. Will that be in the morning or in the afternoon?"
> Dealer: "Sir, it's four years from now."
> Citizen: "I know, but I have a plumber coming in the morning."

Socialism, communism, or any other "ism" that describes a centrally-controlled economy has always, always, always failed. No government bureaucracy, agency, or department could ever hope to run an economy with the same responsiveness or efficiency as occurs in a free market.

Socialism has been tried on our American continent before. When the Pilgrims first landed and began to carve out an existence, they tried collectivism. The food and other resources were shared without regard to how it was produced or who produced what. It was a dismal failure that was nearly fatal for the new colony. Lots of Pilgrims starved to death under this primitive brand of communism. The governor of the colony, William Bradford, documented the results of that experiment in collectivism in his diaries.

> For the young men that were able and fit for labor and service did repine that they should spend their time and strength to work for other men's wives and children, without recompense. The strong,

more of the country's industries. That only served to empty the shelves of basic commodities such as sugar, flour, milk, cooking oil, rice, and even napkins.

Then a series of recurring government actions ensued. First, was the economic crisis—the drop in oil prices. Government steps in to solve the problem. The socialist government seizes property and imposes restrictions and regulations on liberty and free markets. Those actions lead to further problems, such as increased debt. Government comes to the rescue again, this time by printing worthless money, nationalizing more industry, and imposing price controls. Those government actions exacerbate the situation, and crazy inflation rates along with shortages of basic commodities become rampant, leading to empty shelves in supermarkets and long lines for food. These lead to even more government actions. The government did solve the problem of long food lines ... by literally just kicking people out of line! Now the people are assigned positions in the food lines based on the last digits of their national ID cards.

When Dictator Hugo Chavez came into office in 1999, he initiated huge welfare programs. His successor, Nicolas Maduro, has kept these going, only making the government and everyone else poorer.

So the economic death-spiral we are witnessing in Venezuela has gone like this: A socialist dictator takes power, promising everything to everybody and instituting a huge welfare state. The president dictator and his cronies think they can run every aspect of the country's people and economy better than the free market and start to make nonsensical changes. They wrongly try to fix something that wasn't broken, and things go haywire. The economy tanks. Government crushes more liberty and imposes more control. It naturally fails, and things get worse. Government crushes freedom and imposes even more control. Soldiers are deployed to control both food smuggling and the crowds. The *Wall Street Journal* reported 30 percent of Venezuelans eating two or fewer meals a day, and the government is now using fingerprint scanners to track and record food purchases.(4)

Anyone capable of observing events, determining cause and effect, and applying critical-thinking skills would never propose repeating the experience of the Pilgrims or of Venezuela. Does having a massive welfare state that promises everything to everyone while printing huge amounts of money and racking up unsustainable debt, with a steady stream of choking regulations on business, sound familiar? It should; we are doing the exact same thing. I don't know why or how our government thinks the same actions won't lead to the same results. Or even worse, maybe it does know exactly what will happen. If that is the case, we have bigger problems looming over the horizon.

There have been dictatorships, oligarchies, monarchies, state-run economies, and free-market capitalism throughout history in one form or another. You'd figure that by now, we'd be able to judge the outcomes of each of those and determine what has worked and what has not. But we have to share a common sense of what we want the outcome to be. If the desired outcome is for each individual citizen to have the maximum ability to enjoy and the opportunity to achieve prosperity and a better life for future generations, there is really only one choice—a constitutional republic that guarantees maximum liberty for the maximum number of citizens.

Many are saying the Obama administrations have been a failure. Well, that depends. The problem with that analysis is the general assumption that they wanted to achieve the same outcome we want—more jobs, greater prosperity, America in a leadership position in the world, the greatest degree of freedom for our citizens and a general improvement in our standard of living. But if they started out with different goals, we can't judge them a failure by our criteria of success.

If you are looking for an economic and political system that time and again delivers on the stated goals above, look no further than freedom.

> So that the record of history is absolutely crystal clear. That there is no alternative way, so far discovered, of improving the lot of the ordinary people that can hold a candle to the productive activities that are unleashed by a free enterprise system.
>
> —Milton Friedman (5)

When the cultural Marxists first devised their plans to destroy the West, they went right after the most basic of the free citizens' ability to judge right from wrong. They also targeted the schools so they could eliminate critical thinking and problem solving from the curriculum. As Maximilien Robespierre said during the bloody French Revolution, "The secret of freedom lies in educating people, whereas the secret of tyranny is in keeping them ignorant." (6)

America's core institutions are the real threat to the cultural Marxists' objectives. These institutions are the bedrock upon which our entire Western civilization is based. All of these institutions are based on individualism. Our economic system, capitalism, is based on individual hard work, self-motivation, dedication and achievement. Like Thomas Edison said "Genius is one percent inspiration and ninety-nine percent perspiration." Our education system reflects, or at least used to reflect, the same values based on the individual's hard work, study and merit.

It wasn't just education and economics that were the targets. Our culture's most basic core belief system, religion—and specifically, Christianity—had to be driven from our public culture because the teachings of Christianity promoted such values as traditional marriage, individualism, equality, and the basic worth of the human being. Christianity teaches that everyone is a creation of God and therefore equal; it also promotes morality and traditional marriage that produces children in a two-parent household. Equality promotes such political narratives as the rule of law, the concept of the subordination of government to the individual citizen, and private property rights. These ideas are in direct contrast to collectivism. We are seeing now how God is systematically being driven from our schools, courthouses, and public squares. A spiritual people should put their loyalty and faith in God before government. Of course that is a direct contradiction to the collectivist idea that peoples' faith must be in the state. That said, it is the openly-admitted objective of collectivists through socialist-style movements to destroy core institutions so that there is no competition to their new system. A collectivist society cannot allow citizens to have any loyalties beyond their loyalty to the group or the state. To the collectivist, everyone's faith should be in the State, not to God.

There is an even deeper and more sinister reason for the attack on Christianity. As long as citizens believe in God, they also believe they have the ability to judge good from bad and right from wrong. To a Christian, there is an objective good and an objective evil based on the teachings of God and the Bible. The Marxist needs for citizens to surrender their ability to determine right from wrong to the "greater good." That has now become the foundation of political correctness in America.

Nationalism and patriotism are a threat because such ideas promote a shared history, a shared set of values, and a shared national identity and heritage. The Marxist doesn't want us to have any of those because if those ideas are perpetuated from one generation to another, we will be able to identify what is and compare it to what should be as Americans and as a nation. Those ideas must be stripped away. That explains why the Left promotes unrestricted illegal immigration. Allowing millions of non-Americans into the country very quickly dilutes the concepts of national identity and patriotism. This is especially true when there is no expectation that these illegal immigrants will assimilate into an American culture. Instead, we are expected to respect and accept the immigrants' cultures at the expense of our own. To not do so results in being called a racist, xenophobe, or worse. States are now offering driver's licenses to illegal immigrants, and there are federal benefits such as free or subsidized housing, free education, in-state tuition rates for universities, and many more.

There is even a city in California that has allowed two illegal immigrants to become voting members of their city council. The city of Huntington Park, California, has appointed Frank Medina and Julian Zatarain, both in the country illegally, to the town board! (7) Generations of immigrant children are flooding our schools. The level of education Americans receive is dumbed down when teachers struggle to teach because up to half of the kids in their class don't speak English. This will change our culture, our national norms, and our once-shared values, just as intended.

The foundations of our government and American civics are also based on individualism. Our Constitution is a document that places limits on government and spells out guarantees for individual liberty and rights. Through the constant reinterpretation of the Constitution as a "living document," the progressive collectivists strive to diminish or remove our personal liberties and by extension the very worth of the individual citizen. This is done as the government takes on more and more power that it is not afforded in the Constitution and by activist judges who "legislate from the bench." They twist, bend and interpret the Constitution to mean whatever they want it to mean. What we've ended up with is a government that can do anything to anybody for anything. "This," like my dad used to say, "ain't no way to run a railroad."

Last, the most fundamental of our institutions, the family unit, must be broken apart. There are now so many state institutions that pressure the family's demise, it is hard to list them all. Family, child support and visitation laws result in the criminalization of good parents. Entitlement programs reward single parent households over the traditional nuclear family and so much more. The public school system controls the children's morality, language through identity politics, political correctness and statist propaganda.

Speaking of collectivist propaganda, the progressive narrative dominates the political discourse in this country. Through their minions in the media and the politicians, progressive collectivists dictate the national agenda. They tell us what is important and what to pay attention to just by them paying attention to it. For example, every year there is the anti-abortion March for Life in Washington D.C. In 2015 an estimated 500,000 people came to march and call for the end to abortion. (8) The mainstream media didn't cover a minute of it. A half a million people protesting abortion in our nation's capital never made the news. However, when racial protests started on the campus of the University of Missouri, only drawing 40-50 participants in its first days, that event dominated the news for days. (9) President Obama even made a statement praising the student demonstrators. In an interview with ABC News the president said "I want an activist student body just like I want an activist citizenry, and the issue is just making sure that even as these young people are getting engaged, getting involved, speaking out, that they're also listening," he added. "I'd rather see them err on the side of activism than being passive." (10) These protest eventually led to the resignation of the university's president even though he had no control over any of the issues the students were protesting against.

The enemy is also very good at making us believe that there is widespread consensus to their point of view. This is completely artificial. Every day and seemingly from every angle we are constantly bombarded with the collectivist message. Television commercials, Hollywood movies, popular sitcoms, the news, print and social media all broadcast the indoctrination of the cultural Marxist. This message is drafted and funded by a very small and select group of individuals and organizations. From the sheer cacophony of the message and because it permeates every corner of our society, it is easy to assume that if you don't agree, you are the minority.

Consider the issue of climate change for example. Since at least the 1970s we have been hearing how the earth is dying and we are responsible. First it was global cooling and the rising CO2 levels would cause the sun's rays to bounce back into the atmosphere and never strike the earth. This would cause a new ice age. Then it was global warming. The ice caps would melt, sea levels would rise all over the world and we'd all die from our own action.(11) The main spokesman for this movement was collectivist Al Gore. Never mind that after earning millions from spouting his theories the guy saying the oceans would rise then buys a mansion on the beach. I know in my hometown, the winter of 2014 was the coldest recorded in 140 years. Now it's just called "climate change." We hear from the president and other proponents of this myth that "the science is settled." This isn't true at all. Instead those words are supposed to stop all further disagreements with their ideology. This is propaganda by attrition. Even though it is being promoted and spread by a limited number of people, the ideology becomes commonplace. The easiest target to accept this propaganda is our youth through the public school system.

Because the public schools are controlled by government and our kids sitting in them are a captive audience, they're easy pickings when the collectivist looks for targets of propaganda and indoctrination. The youth by their nature are inquisitive and open to new ideas. The cultural Marxists find our schools fertile ground in which to sow their seeds of collectivism.

The theory employed has been called "futurism." The theory, which was a leading philosophy behind the rise of fascism, proclaims that all new ideas are superior in their social usefulness and all old ideas and beliefs should be abandoned. The theory of futurism holds that old and established ideas are now only obstacles to any and all progress to society. Take climate change for example. You'll generally find no stronger adherents to the idea of climate change than in our high schools and colleges. Their left-leaning teachers and professors teach climate change as if it is a generally accepted fact. There is no mention of any dissenting opinion. In these classrooms, questioning whether man-made climate change is real is like questioning whether the sun is real. The kids grow up in the school system just accepting it. "The science is settled." The older generations who question climate change just don't get it. Our ideas are outdated and no longer apply. The end product of this type of indoctrination will be future generations who have always just "known" that made-man climate change is real and threatens our very existence on this planet.

The irony is that the ideas really being embedded into our society through our schools are not new at all. Collectivism, fascism, elitism and totalitarianism are as old as time. Of course, the collectivist would never say any of these words directly, but they are repackaged so each is a crisis that must be addressed. Issues such as institutional racism, oppressed homosexuals, accepting unrestricted immigration and yes, climate change, are all persistent themes. Every day the kids come to class and hear about one oppressed group after another. The cultural Marxists' ideas are pounded into their heads day in and day out until the kids just "know" everything. They "know" that institutional racism and white privilege are used to keep minorities subordinate. The kids "know" that man-made climate change is real and past generations are responsible. They just "know" that transgender people are courageous and have been oppressed by Christian homophobes. I could go on and on and on.

The goal of the cultural Marxist is to mold the world view of this generation and replace all past national values, heritage, national identity and history to fit the collectivist model. They really only have to be successful with one generation. Once that happens, eventually the kids today will turn into the parents of tomorrow. The cultural Marxist collectivist ideas with then be automatically accepted as fact and passed on to future generations. Each generation will accept more and more of their liberty and even their individual identity to be stripped from them, and all in the name of the common good or social justice.

What happens when every kid gets a trophy? It doesn't take too long before they begin to feel entitled. They didn't come to practice any earlier or stay later. They didn't run any extra laps. They didn't even score a single goal, but they "deserve" a trophy. They showed up. Somebody owes them something. This feeling of entitlement without accomplishment leads to sinister ends. Growing up with a combination of a false sense of entitlement and the drumbeat of collectivist ideals results college kids, adults and a society as a whole who believe they are entitled to never be offended.

A world where one can never under any circumstances hear or see any ideas that may be deemed offensive creates an environment of forced silence of any dissenting opinion. A country where only certain viewpoints can ever be expressed turns free individual citizens into a complacent and obedient rabble. Driven by the fear of being ostracized and targeted, the dissenter will often choose silence. Fear is a very powerful tool of the cultural Marxist.

Within such a system, the collectivist seeks the homogenization of society. Individual thought and individual achievement are frowned upon. Individual achievement, the very act of thinking outside of the box by definition require questioning the status quo. Individual thought and an inquisitive mind are the enemies of indoctrination.

This can be seen at work in every institution across America. Schools lower standards so no child is left behind and accommodate the non-English speaking immigrants so kids who can barely read will graduate. Businesses are forced to lower standards in the name of "diversity" while rejecting employees with superior skill sets because they do not belong to a designated victim group. Even our military, the last bulwark of "meritocracy" (a system in which individuals are rewarded and promoted based on performance) have been forced to allow the enlistment of openly-practicing homosexuals and to allow women into combat units like the infantry. Physical standards will of necessity be lowered in the name of "gender parity," putting our Soldiers' lives at risk in the process. In the world of the cultural Marxist, we have to accommodate the lowest common denominator instead of reaching for the highest level of excellence. To not conform is to be attacked. The media will run derogatory stories, you'll be sued, and every power of government will be unleashed against you.

I'll refer to the schools again because they have become pure factories of the collectivist. I had the opportunity to review some 10th grade homework assignments the other day. The task was to write a short original song and perform it in front of the class. The teacher specified the only acceptable subject of the students' songs: how a black character from a story they had read was victimized and oppressed by the white characters. The choice of the book, the choice of the characters, and the forced topic of the students' song all perpetuated the idea of victimhood of protected classes and the vilification of the majority, all strong collectivist ideas and leftist themes.

Our colleges have now become the ground zero for American political correctness. Even admission to the school to begin with became based on gender or nationality or race through programs such as affirmative action. It was as though an oppressed class of citizen deserves entrance into the university at the expense of some member of the perceived oppressor class, even though the excluded student may be more capable. Professors began changing the reading list and excluding writings by dead European males (DEMS) such as Chaucer and Homer and instead assigning readings by authors chosen for their homosexuality, because they are from the third world, or because they are women. (11)

Our campuses now represent the largest concentration of Marxist dogma in the world. It isn't a coincidence that every leftist politician pushes for free college for all Americans. When college is free, more and more of our kids will attend, which helps to promote and disseminate the narrative of the American Left even further. Of course, it also promotes the citizens' dependency on the state. Want to go to college? Meet the right criteria, and the government will provide.

The Frankfurt School was successful in embedding its agenda in our colleges and universities. This is why it was specifically the colleges and college-aged people who led in the counterculture movement of the 1960s. World War II interrupted the plans of the Frankfurt School Marxists. Our fight against the Nazis and Japanese promoted a strong national feeling of patriotism as we rallied around our common cause. But after the war, the children of our greatest generation who fought and won World War II were fair game.

Fast-forward twenty years, and these baby boomers were in college. By then the teachings of the Frankfurt School Marxists had been disseminated throughout our university system. It was working. That generation rebelled against their parents, promoted sexual promiscuity, rejected religion, and took to the streets. The revolution was taking hold.

I turned eighteen in 1985 and joined the Army. After basic and engineer training in Missouri, I was sent off to Germany. I'll spare you the stories of the great German beer and other shenanigans we got into. Most important was that it was still the height of the Cold War, and there I was at the front lines. As a combat engineer unit, if the Russians attacked, our job was to rush to the border with East Germany. We were supposed to blow up stuff, drop landmines, and generally slow down the communist hordes of the Warsaw Pact. We were all ready to do our duty; we didn't expect to really live that long.

From my trips up to the Iron Curtain, I saw for the first time walls built by a government not to keep invaders out but to keep its own people imprisoned inside. I also had the opportunity to visit the concentration camps that remained from the Holocaust. As I walked through the gas chambers and barracks, all the stories and documentaries came to life. Here was the result of an omnipotent state that held the individual as completely expendable. I was proud to wear the uniform of the United States. In front of us was the enemy. It was an enemy that wanted to crush our way of life. They were philosophically the polar opposite of everything our country stood for. We knew that we were the only obstacle in their plan. Standing along that wall, I knew that but for us, there is tyranny.

Fast-forward another fifty years to 2015. The indoctrination of our youth has now become national policy. I took a hiatus from active duty and came home to go to college for a couple semesters as a political science major. I was truly surprised when I listened to my professors. Every day it was another lecture about how evil American corporations were by exploiting the resources of third-world countries or how the American government, backed up by the guns of the military, was oppressing these poor countries. If it weren't for us keeping them down, the world would be a much better place. For the very first time, I was being fed a narrative that was absolutely contrary to everything I had ever learned about America. I was told that our founding fathers were old, rich, white guys who owned slaves and were only trying to feather their own nests, keep themselves wealthy, and so much more. What? *Really?* I couldn't believe what I was hearing! Hadn't these professors ever walked among the graves of our fallen on the beaches of Normandy? Hadn't they seen the barbed wire, guard towers, and minefields built by Big Government all pointed inward ready to kill their own people dare they try to escape? Hadn't they seen the difference between communism and freedom? Didn't they know that America was the greatest force for freedom the world over? Didn't they know that it was America that held the forces of evil and tyranny at bay? No, they didn't know and hadn't done any of those things. They knew what they knew, and there was no disagreeing with them, facts be damned. Dissent was not tolerated.

It's not getting better. If anything, things are taking a significant turn for the worse. The federal government, through the unconstitutional Department of Education, is now imposing Common Core on the country's schoolchildren. They are doing this even though the Constitution does not mention the word education even once. Education is not a power of the federal government; it is exclusively reserved for the states.

By extending or withholding federal education grant funding, the federal government has been able to force states to adopt Common Core standards. What is Common Core? Common Core is a nationalized, one-size-fits-all educational curriculum that is being forced at all levels of our schools. Public schools, private schools, Christian schools, and charter schools will all be forced to adopt this national curriculum.

Why is Common Core so dangerous and insidious to our society? According to Christina Michas, cofounder of Citizens United for Responsible

Education (CURE), "in the Department of Education's own document, 'Grit, Tenacity, and Perseverance,' they outline the data-mining methods that will be used on the children. MRIs will be used through their computers to scan the child to see how they react to different stimuli" (p. 32). Page 44 of the same document shows the different technologies that will be used, such as facial expression cameras that will be on the computer, posture analysis seats, a pressure mouse, and wireless skin conductance sensors. All of these methods, along with the other data collected on families, religious affiliations, voting affiliations, health records, whether or not the families own guns, and so on are just a few of the data points they want to collect from the children. Children will be encouraged to spy and report on what their families do at home. (13)

Just one example of such spying comes from Hendrickson High School in Pflugerville, Texas. Students were issued a questionnaire requiring information on gun ownership, gun usage and even the political views of their parents (14). Among the questions asked were: "Does your family own any guns?" "If so, how many?" "What is their purpose?" It isn't just guns that the administration wants to know about; the questions move onto politics too. "What are your parents' political views?" and "What are your political views?" Why would the school need to know this? Where does that information end up? Do the schools then pass this information up to the state?

Taken all together, it sounds like one of the mentioned "isms" to me. Big Brother will know everything about how you and your children live, work, and play. None of the technology being used has been tested to see what effects, if any, it will have on the children. And if that is not enough, the master teachers will be instructing the teachers to not teach our nation's framework or any form of nationalism. Instead of teaching our proud heritage, they will train students to be "good global, sustainable citizens" prepared for a global world. They will become a managed workforce for the new world order. Many will be forced to choose a career path by the time they are nine years old based on the data mined on each child. Children will be separated based on an analysis of whether they will comply or be rebellious, and they will be placed into groups accordingly. Communist China has this method. The Chinese government decides what career its citizens will have. No longer will a child be able to strive to achieve his or her own goals. The children will be "managed." (15)

"Children will no longer be taught the usual math, literature, history, or social studies," Michas states. "The curriculum, as designed, will change how children learn, as much of our history has been distorted or eliminated by the authors of Common Core. Teachers will teach to the test only. They say that it is to the child's benefit not to teach them critical thinking and problem solving, but rather to memorize desired information; teaching to test only. It will be the dumbing down of our children." (16)

Additionally, there will now be federal master teachers who will come to our schools to train teachers how to properly teach Common Core. These federal agents will also be collecting data on the schools, teachers, and students. This data will be used to grade the schools and teachers on how thoroughly they are indoctrinating the kids with the Common Core standards.

Where did these standards come from? Common Core came from the United Nations, specifically UNESCO. Common Core is part of its global plan, Agenda 21. Michas correctly labels Agenda 21 as the land-grabbing, human suppression, and depopulation program of the United Nations.

I happen to have gone to their schools. When I left the Army, there were several classes available for me to take for free. The training was offered by the US Green Building Council. By taking these classes, I became a certified home energy advisor in leadership in energy efficiency and design (LEED), certified in building design and construction, building operations and maintenance, and LEED homes. Agenda 21 initiatives are heavy throughout all of this instruction. Buildings are rated on such items as having bicycle racks and showers for the employees so the people don't have to have or even own private cars. The building is given a higher LEED score if it has solar power, is close to public transportation, and has grass growing on its roof. Residential buildings and neighborhoods are more desirable if they are close to public transportation again so people don't need their own cars. Most disturbing is that the more people are packed into the smallest space, the higher the score. The goal is to have as many people as possible crammed into as few acres of urban space as possible. Those items are taken directly from the Agenda 21 playbook.

The idea is to depopulate rural areas and migrate everyone into densely packed, urban spaces, then deprive people of their own means of transportation and limit their travel. That's precisely why the government is pushing for high-speed rail and attacking our SUVs and pickup trucks. That—and think about this—is exactly why the narrative of global warming, or climate change, is so absolutely critical to the cultural Marxist's narrative. Everything is justified because we are saving the planet from ourselves! We will be told to move into the urban spaces because, crammed together, we will use less energy, because energy and the resulting CO2 emissions are killing Mother Earth. Yes, the same gas you exhale. We will have to do it anyway because as we kill the use of all fossil fuels, electricity will be too expensive for each of us to afford on our own. I know that to a rational person, this all sounds like far-fetched lunacy, but remember what Barack Obama said in 2008:

> The problem is: can you get the American people to say this is really important and force their representatives to do the right thing? That requires mobilizing a citizenry. That requires them understanding what is at stake. And climate change is a great example. When I was asked earlier about the issue of coal, you know, under my plan, of a cap and trade system, electricity rates will necessarily skyrocket, even, regardless of what I say whether coal is good or bad. Because I'm capping greenhouse gases, coal power plants, natural gas, you name it, whatever the plants were, whatever the industry was, they'll have to retrofit their operations. That will cost money. They will pass that money onto consumers.
>
> Let me sort of describe my overall policy. What I've said is that we would put a cap and trade system in place that is as aggressive if not more aggressive than anybody else's out there. I was the first to call for a 100 percent auction on the cap and trade system. Which means that every unit of carbon or greenhouse gases that was emitted would be

> charged to the polluter. That will create a market in which whatever technology that are out there being presented, whatever power plants are being built, that they would have to meet the rigors of that market and the ratcheted down caps that are in place and imposed every year. So if somebody wants to build a coal powered plant, they can. It's just that it will bankrupt them because they're gonna be charged a huge sum for all that greenhouse gas that is being emitted. (17)

This strict ideology explains why while Obama is visiting Alaska, he sticks to his climate change talking points on global warming. This is despite the fact that it is snowing during his trip in August. Also, Obama ordered new icebreakers for the arctic Coast Guard while simultaneously talking about the ice and glaciers melting at a record pace. It also explains why, as commander in chief, he never even mentions that the Chinese navy sends a contingent of warships through American territorial waters off the Aleutian Islands as an obvious snub of America's weakness. This happened while the president was right there in Alaska. Truth doesn't matter. Facts don't matter. The only thing that matters is pushing forward the cultural Marxist agenda.

The cultural Marxists' list of targets included Hollywood, radio, and our other forms of entertainment. Our entertainment has gone from *Leave It to Beaver* to Miley Cyrus. In a thirty-second television advertisement for a travel website, a homosexual couple is depicted with a baby and a visit to a mosque. The messages are very subtle, but they're there. Television sitcoms routinely depict single parents and gay couples, and the traditional family is no longer the norm. When they do show married households, the male character is generally a dim-witted, effeminate guy whose wife is always correcting him or fixing his mistakes, in opposition to what were once commonly held beliefs regarding the roles of men and women.

In our everyday culture, as described by Michael Minnicino, "The importance of the individual as a person gifted with the divine spark of creativity, and capable of acting upon all human civilization, was replaced by the idea that the person is important because he or she is black, or a woman, or feels homosexual impulses." (18) Recently a high school boy declared he was actually a girl and demanded use of the girls' bathroom and locker room. Many activists and the media immediately called him a hero and referred to the boy as "her" in their reports. "This explains the deformation of the civil rights movement," Minnicino continues, "into a 'black power' movement, and the transformation of the legitimate issue of civil rights for women into feminism." This is why we are seeing movements such as Black Lives Matter receive such attention. Movements that support traditional values, such as the annual March for Life in Washington, receive little or no media attention.

Reason would seem to dictate that successive generations examine what has transpired before and make the necessary adjustments to continuously improve not only their own lives but also this world for their children. By extension, they would be improving society as a whole. As the philosopher Cicero explains in his work, *On Duties*, "But the most marked difference between man and beast is this: the beast, just as far as it is moved by the senses and with very little perception of past or future, adapts itself to that alone which is present at the moment; while man—because he is endowed with reason, by which he comprehends the chain of consequences, perceives the causes of things, understands the relation of cause to effect and of effect to cause, draws analogies, and connects and associates the present and the future—easily surveys the course of his whole life and makes the necessary preparations for its conduct." (19)

We as rational human beings can decipher good from evil, determining the right course of action for most circumstances by examining past cause-and-effect results to see what has worked before and what has failed. The cultural Marxist strives to erase that cognitive thought process. All that matters is the present moment. Everything is based on a perceived system of the oppressed and the oppressors. There is no objective higher moral good or evil by which to judge one's actions.

Objective good and evil have all but disappeared. They have been replaced by the new relativism. Good, evil, right or wrong can only be judged now when the race, economic status, education level and other factors of the people involved are taken into account. I was engaged in a discussion recently about the barbaric actions of the Islamic terror group ISIS. The subject was the crucifixion and murder of children, particularly Christian children in Iraq. When I expressed my utter disgust and said something to the effect that anyone who could do such things has forfeited their right to life. I was shocked by the response. "I'm sure *they* think they're doing the right thing." What?! But, to the modern liberal, everything can be explained away, even the murder of innocent children by nailing them to crosses in front of their families. There is no right or wrong. It wasn't her fault, necessarily, being the product of today's public schools; she was responding in exactly the way she had been taught. This opinion didn't come from a college student influenced by the institutes for social research at Yale, Columbia, Cornell, the University of Michigan or at many, many other colleges across the country, each spouting the same anti-American rhetoric that Theodor Adorno, Herbert Marcuse *or* Walter Benjamin would immediately recognize. No, this came from a high school student. This shows the depth to which the indoctrination of the cultural Marxist has reached into our society.

The for-profit organization Planned Parenthood is caught on video dismembering and selling off the parts of dead babies, yet our government continues to fund it to the tune of over $500 million a year. That means our elected federal representatives are still writing checks using our money to fund the killing of the unborn, even though more than 70 percent of Americans disapprove. In yet another discussion with a different liberal woman and a mother herself, on exactly this issue, she said "well, I'm sure the mothers sign a consent waiver first." So, that makes it ok? Evil becomes good, ignored or at least tolerated and everything good becomes evil.

Thousands of Christians are murdered in the Middle East in what can only be described as genocide, and the media barely pays any attention at all. Even while our soldiers are still serving and dying in Afghanistan, anyone who shows the slightest dissent against Muslims is immediately called an Islamophobe and the ever-prevalent racist. As I write this, 129 innocent French citizens were just murdered in Paris in a well-coordinated attack on Friday the 13th of November 2015. The initial investigation has determined that the terrorists planned their attack in Syria and that at least some of the perpetrators came into France as Syrian "refugees." Evan after these gruesome attacks, our president has called for the United States to take in more Syrian refugees and assured the countries of Europe that America would help pay for them to take in more Syrian refugees too. Also, the president released five prisoners from Guantanamo Bay detention camp in Cuba in the same weekend. There is an outright cultural Marxist refusal to attribute these attacks to the terrorist group or its Islamic religious motivations.

Isolation, name-calling, assigning guilt, and silencing dissent are the product of our politically correct society, which was the goal of the Frankfurt School. For at least three generations, the narrative instilled into our higher education—and then, as these students graduated, into our politics and media—has been tolerance. That means tolerance of everything that contradicts traditional values, our history, common sense, and spirituality. Anything else must be silenced. If you are against illegal immigration, you are a racist. If you are against the policies of President Obama, you're a racist. If you say all lives matter, you're a racist. If you don't agree that climate change is real and manmade, you're a denier. If you use pronouns that distinguish between males and females, you're using hateful language or speaking "micro-aggressions." It's enough to make your head explode!

The statesman Edmund Burke wrote of the same kind of philosophy way back in 1757 in his article titled "A Vindication of Natural Society." In it, he said, "The design was, to shew that, without the exertion of any considerable forces, the same engines which were employed for the destruction of religion, might be employed with equal Success for the Subversion of Government; and that specious arguments might be used against those things which they, who doubt of everything else, will never permit to be questioned." (20) He meant that those who seek to use fallacious arguments to destroy what we know to be right will never accept intelligent challenge. Those promoting the leftist agenda now in America likewise seek to silence all dissent because they cannot support their arguments through reason.

In many of our universities, there are "free speech zones," which are the only spaces from which a student is allowed to voice dissent. However, those speaking in favor of the cultural Marxist agenda are free to hold rallies or speak out wherever they like. The situation has gotten much worse in our universities even since I started this work.

As of late, spurred on by the Black Lives Matter movement, college students have taken to declaring victimhood amid widespread institutional racism inherently present on our campuses. Evidence of such racism isn't needed. These kids are entitled to live their lives with no chance of ever being offended so anything they say must be taken seriously and this must stop. Now schools like the University of Missouri, as we've discussed, Ithaca College and even Princeton have black student safe spaces where there is no chance they'll be victims of any viewpoint, idea or opinion with which they may disagree.

Allow me a moment to clarify something. Yes, I mention the racist Black Lives Matter movement (any movement based solely on race is by definition racist). Before I get mislabeled as a racist, let me ask a question: What was the racial makeup of the "multitude" present when Jesus distributed the loaves and fishes? I don't know either, because it didn't matter. We are all created equal with equal worth and equal rights.

Our world has been turned upside down. Everything that was good is now bad, and everything evil is now to be tolerated. Tolerance, however, is only a one way street. We must tolerate whatever the Left dictates while, again, any dissent must be silenced. Tolerance doesn't mean what you think. In today's political parlance, tolerance means embracing, not criticizing, and accepting not only the new moral standards but the outright disregard and discarding of the old, now outdated morals and value systems. That is the new definition of tolerance.

This isn't an accident. The turmoil we have seen in our cities, from the increase in crime, with flash mobs looting stores, to the riots in Ferguson, MO, and Baltimore, MD, is a direct result of the Frankfurt School style of cultural Marxism. It was designed to corrupt the young, get them away from religion, encourage their interest in sex, make them superficial by focusing their attention on sensual entertainment, and then craft the entertainment to promote messages promoting the destruction of our culture. It preaches tolerance while silencing any opposition to its agenda, encouraging government spending and extravagance along with a breakdown of morality and cultural norms by creating victim classes. Then it pits these classes against everything of our traditional culture.

Has it worked? The proof is everywhere. Michael Snyder, in *Investment Watch*, published an article titled "40 Signs That We Have Seriously Messed Up the Next Generation of Americans." (21) In it, he describes many of the social and even physical effects that cultural Marxism, masked as political correctness, has had in our current generation of American kids. Among them are skyrocketing rates of STDs, broken families, physical ailments, national debt, teen pregnancy, and many others. Remember, the kids he described in his 2012 article are the adults and parents of tomorrow. It is equally important to remember that this wasn't an accident or a result of poor policy. It was by design.

This agenda has recently even been codified by the Supreme Court. Take, for example, the ruling on Obamacare. No matter how this law is analyzed, it is unconstitutional. Can the government compel private citizens to purchase a product? No. The government is not granted that power in the Constitution. The Supreme Court ruled that it can. Can the government impart financial penalties on a private citizen for failing to purchase a product? No such power in the Constitution is designated to the federal government for that either. The Supreme Court instead ruled that all penalties were in fact a tax. Ok, so it's a tax, despite what the text of the actual law says. If it is a tax, the law is unconstitutional. According to Article I of the Constitution, all bills for generating revenue must start in the House of Representatives. Obamacare started in the Senate and is therefore, again, unconstitutional. But it is the law.

The Supreme Court also ruled that same-sex marriage is legal in all fifty states. Where in the Constitution does the word "marriage" occur? It doesn't. Therefore the ruling and any accompanying laws are unconstitutional.

The saddest part about all of the recent Supreme Court decisions, especially the gay marriage ruling, is how liberals are using these issues to divide us. A people divided against itself is simply easier to control. That's the point. In a famous case, a Christian bakery refused to bake a cake for a same-sex wedding ceremony. The couple requesting the cake had been customers of the bakery for some time, and the Christian bakers never refused to sell them their products. Only when they were asked to provide the cake for the wedding ceremony, with which they disagreed on religious grounds, did the bakers refuse. The media and legal backlash were immediate. These Christian bigots and religious zealots were suddenly, according to the gay activists and the media, forcing their religion on others. The couple was forced to close the business, and the court fined them $135,000. That is what this country has become.

It is similar to the whole Black Lives Matter campaign in the news and on our streets as of late. Do you think the Democrats—the party of slavery, the party that founded the KKK after the Civil War and established, promoted, and perpetuated segregation, the party with prominent members of the Senate also serving as grand dragons in the KKK, the party that filibustered civil rights legislation in the 1950s and 1960s, the party of Margaret Sanger, who founded Planned Parenthood to spread abortion as a means to control and eliminate minority races in the United States—now suddenly cares about race? No, far too many of them owe their living to perpetuating racial issues. There are too many politicians who count on divisive and racial politics for their reelection and their retaining power.

It is the same on the same-sex marriage issue. So we're to believe that the Democrat party in control of the military and foreign affairs is celebrating this SCOTUS decision while remaining absolutely silent on the hundreds if not thousands of homosexuals being murdered by ISIS and throughout the Islamic world? They suddenly care about gay marriage? They don't. They care *only* about power and control. Lyndon B. Johnson said, when he signed welfare into law in 1964, "We'll have those ni**gers voting Democrat for two hundred years." (22) Incidentally, this is the same party that booed God and by voice-vote kicked God out of its platform three times at its convention.

This party's goal is to divide us while simultaneously destroying every foundation this country was built on—Christianity, religious freedom, and family, turning us into a rabble. In a democracy, the majority can vote away the rights of the minority. In a democracy, your neighbors can hold a vote to sell your house and divide up the proceeds.

We are, or at least were supposed to be, a republic in which the government, with limited powers, exists primarily to protect our rights—everyone's rights equally.

The same-sex marriage ruling will be used to attack anyone who protests or even disagrees. Now, activists will sue and use the power of the state to force churches that disagree to perform ceremonies that oppose their religious beliefs. Activists have already successfully sued and used the power of the state to force businesses that proclaim religious objections to abandon their beliefs and conform and obey.

Would the state similarly use the power of force to compel an African American–owned restaurant to cater and serve at a KKK banquet? Would the state force a Jewish-owned business to cater and serve at a Nazi rally?

I have to bring up another point here on this debate. The fact that the Supreme Court makes a ruling doesn't make the ruling a law. Yes, the Supreme Court ruled that same-sex marriage is legal. This means that if and when Congress or a state legislature passes a law allowing same-sex marriage, that law passes judicial review. The other side of the coin is that if Congress or a state legislature were to pass a law prohibiting same-sex marriages, that law would be illegal. The ruling, in and of itself, is not a law. Court rulings on matter of law are, or at least used to be, "opinions" and not rulings. The courts don't rule over us, either. They offer their opinions on matters of law. They neither make nor enforce law. Justices cannot speak law.

I know there has been disagreement on this point. Article III in section 2 of the Constitution spells out the jurisdiction of the Supreme Court as follows:

> The judicial Power shall extend to all Cases, in Law and Equity, arising under this Constitution, the Laws of the United States, and Treaties made, or which shall be made, under their Authority;—to all Cases affecting Ambassadors, other public Ministers and Consuls;—to all Cases of admiralty and maritime Jurisdiction;—to Controversies to which the United States shall be a Party;—to Controversies between two or more States;—between a State and Citizens of another State,—between Citizens of different States,—between Citizens of the same

> State claiming Lands under Grants of different States, and between a State, or the Citizens thereof, and foreign States, Citizens or Subjects.

In September 2015, a county clerk in Kentucky, Kim Davis, was jailed for five days for refusing to issue marriage licenses to same-sex couples. (23) A judge ruled that her actions are in violation of the Supreme Court ruling on gay marriage and issued his own court order for her to issue the licenses. She still refused based on her religious convictions. However true that may be, the real legal argument is that she is not in violation of any law because there is no federal law to codify or back up the court's opinion. Therefore, she has broken no law. In fact, whereas the word "marriage" does not appear in the Constitution at all, any federal ruling on anyone's marriage, gay or straight, is unconstitutional. The state constitution of Kentucky specifically prohibits gay marriage.

The state constitutional amendment, passed in 2004, reads, "Only a marriage between one man and one woman shall be valid or recognized as a marriage in Kentucky. A legal status identical or substantially similar to that of marriage for unmarried individuals shall not be valid or recognized." By not issuing marriage licenses, not only is this county clerk *not* in violation of any law, but she is acting in accordance with her state's law. In my opinion, her arrest was illegal. Unless and until the US Constitution and the state constitution of Kentucky are amended, that would change the law, there is no law for Ms. Davis to break. That is just one example of how the federal government, acting illegally and unconstitutionally, infringes on our rights and state sovereignty.

I have read and reread the Constitution regarding the Supreme Court's powers, and I may be mistaken, but I don't see anything that grants it power to make law.

In a republic, the rule of law is supreme. The first step, or maybe the last step in "fundamentally transforming" America from a republic respecting rights, limited government, and the rule of law is to turn us against ourselves and use the power of the state to proclaim the lie that we have to abandon our rights to protect our rights. This transforms us into a rabble driven by the propaganda of the state, broadcasted by the state-controlled media. Thus, little by little, we sacrifice everything to save something that they are taking away from us regardless.

There is a very obvious selective application of the law in America. If you happen to break the law, but you're doing it supporting the cultural Marxist agenda, you're likely to be ignored. Take once again the issue of same-sex marriage. Whatever your views are on the issue, I think we can agree the rule of law should prevail. Not so fast. You'd think that if a clerk was sent to jail for illegally *refusing to issue* marriage licenses, then if a clerk was illegally *issuing* marriage licenses, that clerk would also go to jail. Nope. Not if the clerk was illegally issuing same-sex marriage licenses. In 2004, the mayor of San Francisco ordered his city clerk to issue same-sex marriage licenses, in clear violation of the then-existing law. In about a month, more than four thousand illegal licenses were issued. If we are a nation of law, someone should have gone to jail. No one went to jail.

If we were a nation of law, then you'd think that if a number of US cities decided on their own to ignore federal law, someone would be held accountable and be either fined or jailed, right? Well, that depends. If those cities are promoting policies in support of the cultural Marxist agenda, nothing will happen. Right now there are 340 cities across America that provide shelter to illegal immigrants. These "sanctuary cities," are where illegal immigrants know they are very unlikely to face prosecution or deportation. (24) Offering sanctuary to criminals, and illegal immigrants by definition are criminals, as the administration of these cities are doing, is in clear violation of federal law. The selective enforcement and application of law is the very definition of tyranny. If law can be either enforced or ignored based on the political motives of the perpetrator and the enforcer, we no longer have law.

Unfortunately, and purposefully, today's generation has been trained to feel, not to think. They have been trained to be so indiscriminate they can no longer tell right from wrong by any objective measure. They have been trained by our government-run schools and universities to emotionally respond to the issues presented to them by the state and have no logical critical-thinking skills, historical perspective, or real education in civics to compare and contrast what is happening versus what is supposed to be. So they jump on the bandwagon to call anyone who opposes the state's agenda "haters" and "bigots" with no perspective beyond what the cultural Marxist's lessons from their government-run schools tell them to feel.

That is precisely what the agenda of the new Common Core federally-mandated curriculum is about. Creating generations of Americans who are taught what to think and not how to think is necessary for their agenda. So we are now in an America where if a sports figure undergoes gender reassignment surgery, he/she is hailed as a hero. Yet there are marches in the streets calling for the murder of our police officers and demonstrations at our colleges demanding the resignation of their school's presidents. What in the world has happened to us?

The answers to what ails America, and by extension the world, can all be found in the teachings of God and the Bible. Within the Word lie the subtle and sometimes not-so-subtle guidelines that spell out how a free and prosperous society is built. And like it or not, America is the world's most influential country. Since at least the end of World War II, the United States has been the leader of the free world. Millions have willingly risked not only their own lives but also the lives of their children to reach our shores and freedom.

But where does that freedom come from? How is America different, and how did we become that way? There must be something different, exceptional even, that would in such a short period, relative to other countries, propel a country so far forward.

Our Declaration of Independence listed our unalienable rights as life, liberty, and the pursuit of happiness. We'll roughly follow that formula here. Any society is constructed of building blocks—the individual, the family, the neighborhood and community, the state, and then the country. If the foundation, the individual and family, is rotten, the whole structure disintegrates. That is what we are witnessing right now in America. Our families are crumbling because we no longer believe in or behave according to the roles laid out for us as husbands and wives, and therefore fathers and mothers. If our families are a mess, our kids will be too. Then how can we expect our neighborhoods and communities to be free, law abiding, and prosperous when within the homes that make up that community we find such strife, tension, and misery?

You can see where this is going.

America is an exceptional country. That isn't a very politically correct statement right now, but America really is special. What makes us special is how we were put together. I don't mean geographically; I refer to the reasons people came here in the first place and the institutions we built to preserve and protect us as we pursue our dreams. All of that comes from what used to be our generally held beliefs that nothing is more important or valuable than the individual citizen. Times have changed.

America's founding principles used to be grounded on faith, family, and freedom. Now it seems that if you still stand for those convictions, you're standing alone. Sometimes it can make you feel that the whole world has been turned upside down. Do you often feel as though you are the one rock in the current trying to hold back the flood?

You're not alone. Millions of Americans feel exactly as you do. It is our national character, and there is a reason for this. When our founders purposefully put this country together, they used Christian-Judeo values as the foundation. Why?

If you believe in God, you must believe in freedom. It really is that simple. Christ's teachings were of faith, tolerance, peace, and, yes, liberty. It would be impossible to "love your brother as yourself" and then believe you should rule over them. It would be impossible to infringe upon their rights through force and the rule of law and still believe you are both still equals in the eyes of God.

> **Galatians 5:13** For you were called to freedom, brothers. Only do not use your freedom as an opportunity for the flesh, but through love serve one another.

God is not an American God. But America was the first nation on earth founded on Christian-Judeo values and God's freedom. It has been our national tradition and heritage since our founding. The first settlers who came to this land were specifically seeking religious freedom. In that way, America stands for something different and better than the rest of the world.

Christians have especially been under a lot of stress lately. It seems that every social ill is suddenly attributed to intolerant, bigoted, and homophobic Christians.

As Pastor Chuck Baldwin puts it, "Can we not see that what is at stake is the preservation of religious liberty and Christian conscience in our land? Radical secularists (and even some anti-Christian religionists) desire to expunge every semblance of Christian thought and ideology from our nation. The purge has already begun." (25)

Chuck is absolutely right. That is precisely why this book is written. But there's more. What is the motivation behind this anti-Christian movement?

It is plainly evident that darkness is on the march. The goal of the Left and the cultural Marxist is to control or remove every institution in our community that lies between the individual and the state. These priceless institutions include our faith, family, teachers and schools, history, and just about everything else you can think of.

They are attacking God and religion most vigorously because our Christian faith teaches us that God is supreme—not man, and certainly not a government created by man. God is love. A nation with God's love and God's law as its foundation will of necessity be free. That is why the forces of darkness pursue us so greedily. But they have to convince us of something sinister first.

They have to convince you that you are worthless. You have no value. That is what the statist, the enemy, will have you believe. Human beings having no intrinsic value greater than their corporal body is an imperative to their achieving their agenda goals. The statist believes that the state is omnipotent and the people exist to serve government. Therefore, the concept of citizen doesn't apply in the traditional sense that corresponds with our national heritage.

Our American national heritage, however, suggests something completely different. The Declaration of Independence, America's first founding document, proposed what at the time was a radical ideal:

> We hold these truths to be self-evident, that all men are created equal, that they are endowed by their Creator with certain unalienable Rights, that among these are Life, Liberty and the pursuit of Happiness. That to secure these rights, Governments are instituted among Men, deriving their just powers from the consent of the governed.

Where did this radical idea come from? For thousands of years prior to the American experience, people were ruled by kings, emperors, and tyrants. Laws were created at the whim of the pharaoh. The rabble, the "masses," held no individual intrinsic value above how they could serve the state. As such, people could be sold into slavery, whipped, imprisoned, or killed at the word of the king or the state.

The concept that human beings are creations of God implies that we have a greater value than just our mortal bodies.

> **Genesis 1:27** God created man in His own image, in the image of God He created him; male and female He created them.

If that is true, if we all are God's creations, we are created equal. If we are created equal, no one has a right to rule over anyone except at the consent of the governed, and even then, only temporarily.

The recent attacks we see on Christianity are nothing less than an attack on the basic premise that there is a God, and we are created in His image. It is an attack on the basic premise that we are all created equal and endowed by our Creator with our rights.

We derive our worth from God. It is God who endows us with rights. All human beings are equal because we are all creations of God. This belief that we are all equal is why the rule of law is critical. No one is above the law because we are all equal. The law applies equally to everyone. Out of necessity, we as a free and equal people created a government. Or as stated in the Declaration of Independence, "That to secure these rights, Governments are instituted among Men." So government exists only to secure our God-given rights.

To successfully rule over us, statists must first remove God from the equation. That is what is at the root of the current attack against Christians and Christianity. Statists must lower the value of the individual citizen such that we become serfs. That is what made America different at our founding. Royalty asserts that the king is more valuable than those ruled. We based our system of government on Christian values that asserted that everyone is equal; citizens choose their government at the consent of the governed.

We are witnessing a widespread attack on these Christian values and beliefs. God is being systematically removed from our schools, courthouses, and legislatures. Christian-owned businesses are under attack from every angle and being forced to either compromise their beliefs or shut down their businesses. Our pastors and ministers are threatened with losing their tax-exempt status if they do not comply with the state's interpretation of God's marriage. Bible publishers are being sued to remove verses from the Bible, with the demand that scriptures condemning sodomy be eviscerated.

If our rights come from government and not God, then the government can take them away. Conversely, if there is no God, then the supremacy of the rule of law no longer applies because we are no longer equal before the law or the courts. The law can be amended, applied, or suspended at the whim of the state. This is the definition of tyranny. Our equality and our rights are likewise at the whim of the state.

If the movement to remove God from our public square, public discourse, schools, and courts is successful, then our rights no longer come from God but from government. And with no God, humans have no soul and therefore no value above that of a worm, a skunk, or a chicken. We're all just animals. We are reduced to servants of the state.

No other political concept has had such a profound impact on our collective policy as the mythical "separation of church and state." The concept that religion and politics shall forever remain completely separated has codified itself in practice and in law. Today, this metaphor has been used to drive all remnants of God, faith, and religion from all public discussion. Atheist groups have sued to have postings of the Ten Commandments removed from courthouses and public schools, crosses from veterans' memorials, and more every day. Prayer in school is now largely prohibited. Students have been punished for simply reading the Bible or even saying "Bless you" after a fellow student sneezes. For example, Kendra Turner was ejected from her class and received in-school suspension for doing just that at Dyer County High School in Dyersburg, Tennessee. When her teacher called her out for responding with "God bless you" when another student sneezed, Kendra stated that she had a First Amendment right. "I stood up and said, 'My pastor said I have a constitutional right—First Amendment freedom of speech,'" Kendra later wrote on Facebook, and her teacher responded, "Not in my class you don't." (26)

In another case, 12 year old Giovanni Rubeo was reading the Bible during reading free time in his class at Park Lakes Elementary School in Fort Lauderdale, Florida. When the teacher saw that he was reading the Bible, she had him go to the front of the room in front of the other students and call his parents. No one answeredso she left a voicemail syaing "I noticed that he has a book – a religious book – in the classroom. He's not permitted to read those books in my classroom." (27)

There's many other such cases of the public schools shutting down any signs of Christianity in the school system going back for years. In September 2006, seventh grader Amber Magnum was quietly reading the Bible when the vice principle at Dwight D. Eisenhower Middle School in Laurel, Maryland told her to stop or "face punishment." (28) Then there is the case of Joshua Patterson in Plainview, Texas. He was again quietly reading the Bible during recess. He was warned to stop practicing his religion. When he did not comply, the Plainview Middle School suspended the 13 year old boy. Daniel Patterson, Joshua's father was rightfully furious. "We are going to fight this with all of our might," said the child's father Daniel Patterson. "How can a school tell a student that something as simple as reading his Bible is wrong? This school has violated the rights of our child," Mr. Patterson continued "and we will ensure this never happens to another student." (29)

Religion in general, and Christianity in particular, are under attack in America like never before. Christian-owned businesses have been sued, fined, and forced to close their doors for standing up for their religious rights. Lawsuits abound attacking everything from war memorials, 9/11 crosses and veteran memorials, to prayers and even the mention of anything religious in the public square. Most often the separation of church and state is used as justification for expelling God and religion. Hypocritically, it has been the excuse used repeatedly to allow the state to rule on religion.

But where does the very concept of separation of church and state come from? It is nowhere in the Constitution. Government is prohibited from establishing a state religion and from passing laws that would prohibit anyone's free practice of any religion. But there is no prohibition against the involvement of religion in politics. I'll talk about the Bill of Rights more in a while, but let me just mention this here.

The First Amendment reads as follows:

> Congress shall make no law respecting an establishment of religion, or prohibiting the free exercise thereof; or abridging the freedom of speech, or of the press; or the right of the people peaceably to assemble, and to petition the Government for a redress of grievances.

Again, the state is prohibited from getting involved in religion and guarantees citizens' rights to worship. It does not prohibit religion from being involved in politics or the display or expression of anything religious in the public square. So where does the concept of this separation of church and state originate?

It dates back to October 7, 1801, when the Danbury Baptist Association of Connecticut wrote to President Thomas Jefferson. The association was concerned about the state's legislature in its religious affairs. The Baptists felt that the free practice of their religion was at the behest of the state, which was violating their rights to freely exercising their religion. While acknowledging that Jefferson could not legislate on the matter, they expressed the wish that his views on religious liberty "shine and prevail through all these states and all the world."

Thomas Jefferson provided a quick response to the association asserting his belief that the state had no business involving itself in the affairs of the Danbury Baptist Association of Connecticut or any other religious group:

> Believing with you that religion is a matter which lies solely between Man & his God, that he owes account to none other for his faith or his worship, that the legitimate powers of government reach actions only, and not opinions, I contemplate with sovereign reverence that act of the whole American people which declared that their legislature should "make no law respecting an establishment of religion, or prohibiting the free exercise thereof," thus building a wall of separation between Church and State. Adhering to this expression of the supreme will of the nation in behalf of the rights of conscience, I shall see with sincere satisfaction the progress of those sentiments which tend to restore to man all his natural rights, convinced he has no natural right in opposition to his social duties. (30)

Jefferson's use of the words "a wall of separation between Church and State" has been twisted by activist judges and antireligious groups to mean anything they want it to mean. The judiciary has used Jefferson's words as a bludgeon to attack religion since the case of *Everson v. Board of Education* in 1947. "In the words of Jefferson," the justices famously declared, the First Amendment "was intended to erect 'a wall of separation between church and State'...[that] must be kept high and impregnable. We could not approve the slightest breach."

They were only half right. The state cannot infringe on anyone's right to worship as they choose. The state cannot establish any official religion. However, there is no prohibition against religion being practiced in the public square, in public schools, or in city hall. Pastors can speak and sermonize regarding any topic they so choose, to include politics. No one forfeits their First Amendment rights as they enter the public space or the congregation.

Some people may be offended by that. Too bad. Among all the rights guaranteed to us by the Bill of Rights, the right to not be offended is not one of them. Remember, your freedom to be you also includes my freedom to be free from you. In other words, to twist a freedom and right into a power to impose your will on another is hypocritical.

But that is not what this book is about. As Christians, it is important that we know we are not alone. We must keep our faith despite the pressure to compromise and despite the worst this world can throw at us. What is faith? Faith is more than knowing that God and Jesus Christ exist. It is more than believing His Word. It is an assurance that in the end, everything will be all right, and God has plans and desires for our lives.

Light will prevail over darkness. But it won't happen all by itself. That's where you and I come in. Matthew West wrote a beautiful song called "Do Something":

> I woke up this morning
> Saw a world full of trouble now
> Thought, how'd we ever get so far down
> How's it ever gonna turn around
> So I turned my eyes to Heaven
> I thought, "God, why don't You do something?"
> Well, I just couldn't bear the thought of
> People living in poverty
> Children sold into slavery
> The thought disgusted me
> So, I shook my fist at Heaven
> Said, "God, why don't You do something?"
> He said, "I did; I created you." (31)

We have to be the change we want to see. We can do it. We *must* do it. God has a plan, and there is a reason you are here now. You are not alone, and together, "with a firm reliance on the protection of divine Providence" we can still save the country and change the world. It is high time the good guys won one.

# 3

# Big Government, Little Citizen

**"A government big enough to give you everything you want, is strong enough to take everything you have."**

**— Thomas Jefferson**

Almost every other country in the world is older than the United States. Some have existed, if not by the same name, at least with essentially the same people and in the same location for thousands and thousands of years. How are these countries doing in comparison to America?

I watched a television show in which the host visited Mozambique in East Africa the other night. Mozambique sits near where science believes man as a species originated. It's right around where the stick figures on the evolutionary scale straightened their backs and became Homo Sapiens for the first time. So if any region in the world has had a head start on the rest of us, it would be there. If you go there now, it is a rundown, economically struggling country. Mud huts, no electricity, no running water, inadequate medical facilities, and practically a nonfunctioning education system. It is a third-world hole.

I served three tours in Iraq. On the banks of the Tigris and Euphrates, Iraq is the cradle of civilization. So Iraq was a civilization for thousands of years before the founding of America too. If you were to visit Iraq with no information other than that they have been there for thousands and thousands of years, you'd probably expect to find a highly advanced country. Instead, you'd find a very poor country with limited infrastructure and medical care, poor schools, and subsistence farming. It is a country plagued with never-ending violence, organized crime, corruption at every level of government when that government functions at all, and currently an invasion by a gruesome army of murderous Islamists, ISIS.

So, what made the United States different? We've been a country only since the end of the Revolutionary War in 1783, a scant 232 years. By comparison, we are babes in the scope of global history. How did we advance so far so quickly? The answer is found in the principles held by the Founders and Framers who put our great country together.

> It is a maxim that in every government, there must exist, somewhere, a supreme, sovereign, absolute, and uncontrollable power; but this power resides always in the body of the people; and it never was, or can be, delegated to one man, or a few; the great Creator has never given to men a right to vest others with authority over them, unlimited either in duration or degree.
>
> —Alexander Hamilton

It is important to note that man cannot delegate to government any power that we don't ordinarily possess ourselves. Just as you can't go into a bank and plunder all of the cash for any reason, even to give it to a homeless shelter, you cannot empower the government to do it on your behalf. Doing so would violate the owners of the bank and the depositors their right to be secure in their property. To convince the mayor or the city council to pass a law forcing the bank to transfer all of its cash to the homeless shelter is no less a crime against the bank and against God. It is, in fact, worse than doing it yourself because the bank would depend on its government, through the court, to redress the wrong committed against it. When it is done by the government, to whom can they turn for help?

"Man is capable of knowing many things about God," John Locke said in his "An Essay Concerning Human Understanding" in 1689. Locke reasoned "The Creator must of necessity be a cogitative (reasoning or thinking) being, for man is a cogitative (reasoning) being. Certainly a noncogitative being, such as a rock, could never have produced a cogitative being such as a man. We may also know that the divine Creator has a sense of compassion and love, for he gave mankind these sublime qualities."

The Creator would also reflect a fine sense of right and wrong, as well as a sense of indignation or even anger with those who violate the laws of right action. In other words, God has a strong sense of justice. Remorse for wrong also arouses a sense of compassion in the Creator, just as it does in human beings whom He designed.

There are other attributes of man that human beings must necessarily share with their Creator if man is made in the image of God. One is a sense of humor. The Creator must also be a great artist on the visual plane. Everything the Creator organizes is beautiful through color, form, and contrasts. Obviously, man can enjoy only to a finite degree the capacity of his Creator to appreciate the vast panorama of sensory satisfaction that we call beauty.

So, as John Locke said, there are many things man can know about God. And because any thoughtful person can gain an appreciation and conviction of these many attributes of the Creator, Locke felt that anyone who calls himself an atheist has failed to apply his divine capacity for reason and observation.

The American founding fathers agreed with Locke. They considered the existence of the Creator the most fundamental premise underlying *all* self-evident truth. It will be noted as we proceed through this study that every single self-evident truth enunciated by the founders is rooted in the presupposition of a divine Creator.

America has absolutely been blessed. We have abundant natural resources, defensible borders guarded on two sides by vast oceans, and a stable government. But that isn't all that made us what we became. There's something more fundamental to account for our success, something more basic that speaks to who we are, or at least who we once were as a people, and that first defined us and then allowed us to prosper. It was our nearly universally held belief in God.

If you examine the rise and decline of other nations throughout human history, what you'll find is a history wrought with tyranny. The normal course of events is one of humans being ruled by a king, pharaoh, junta, or some other form of dictatorship. Think of it. Every single person who perpetrated the Holocaust or the Armenian genocide, everyone who shipped people off to the gulags of the Soviet Union or to the killing fields in Cambodia or even cut the hearts out of living victims on the Aztec pyramids, was a government employee. Every one of them. The fundamental difference is the value those governments placed on the individual citizen.

If you believe that people have no value beyond being servants to the state, you can do anything to them as long as your actions advance the agenda or expand the power of the State. The people become cannon fodder for wars of expansion. "The rabble," or "the masses" only exist at all to serve the purposes of and at the whim of government. Using Mozambique again as an example, when the communists took power in 1975, their first act was to outlaw religion. Why?

During the Soviet Revolution, the communists seized church property and forbade churches from operating schools or publishing any religious publications. They likewise forbade churches from operating health care institutions or providing aid through organized charity, ministry for justice, or works of mercy that flow naturally from a living faith. All of these prohibitions were conducted by the government. Bishops and priests were imprisoned and even executed.

The communists didn't outright outlaw religion, but they had no use for it either. Lenin called all religion "the opiate of the masses" and expected faith in God to die of its own accord with the institution of the all-powerful State.

In fact, the Communist Party of the Soviet Union (CPSU) issued the ABCs of Communism in 1919 under Lenin and Trotsky, stating what they thought would be the natural end of religion and faith:

> The transition from the society which makes an end of capitalism to the society which is completely freed from all traces of class division and class struggle, will bring about the natural death of all religion and all superstition.(1)

The point is that when people seek to rule over others, every institution that lies between the individual person and the state is a threat. God is chief among them. The tyrant can't have the masses worshiping both God and the state, even if the state is embodied in one person, so God has to go. If you're the dictator, you have to be The Man. That's why tyrants such as Hitler, Gaddafi in Libya, Mao, and Stalin all have to be rock stars. Their pictures are everywhere—in the town squares, classrooms, courthouses, you name it, even in the churches, when houses of worship are still allowed to exist. Everyone from new military recruits to new government employees and even Boy Scouts (Hitler Youth) first swear fidelity and loyalty not to a Constitution or to God but to the ruler or the party. It is a total cult of personality. Everything good suddenly is due to their new "god," whether it is Pol Pot or Xerxes. Everything bad is someone else's fault, just like the Democrats are still blaming George W. Bush for everything, for example.

The young are the easiest to indoctrinate. That's why academia, from elementary school to the university, was among the cultural Marxists' first targets. Our founders knew that to preserve liberty, God and religion must remain in our schools. "The only foundation for a useful education in a republic is to be aid in religion," remarked Benjamin Rush, signer of the Declaration of Independence. "Without this there can be no virtue, and without virtue there can be no liberty, and liberty is the object and life of all republican governments. Without religion, I believe that learning does real mischief to the morals and principles of mankind." (2) The Left, the cultural Marxists, are doing all they can to ensure that our schools are not an aid in religion.

What follows next for that society has been repeated over and over throughout history. Government becomes omnipotent in people's lives and controls everything. The people become property of the state. As the government tries to do, be, and control everything, it expands. There are bureaucracies, departments, and agencies on top of bureaucracies, departments, and agencies. Anything that the citizen has to do—start a business, get a loan, go to college, buy a home, dig a well, everything—requires stacks of government forms to be filled out and multiple visits to this office or that department, often resulting in hours standing in line.

Then corruption creeps in at every level. People who enjoy absolute control have absolute power over the people. The relationship between the citizen and the government gets turned upside down. Because you *have* to get this or that bureaucrat's blessing to do something, these unelected bureaucrats soon start to think that you work for them. No longer are they public servants. We become "the rabble." It doesn't take long before these people realize that their approval alone becomes a commodity that desperate people will pay money to receive. Want a signature? Pay me. Want to cut in line and not wait two years for a building permit? Pay me.

I was in Baghdad in the exceedingly hot summer of 2005. One afternoon, my cultural advisor and translator and I walked into the Council of Ministers' building in the green zone. Sadly I can't remember her name. She was a fearless Chaldean Christian American woman with family in Iraq. We travelled some very dangerous roads throughout my tour and she never flinched. Still wearing my bulletproof vest and ammo pouches, I took off my Kevlar advanced combat helmet and confidently walked up to the receptionist. The building was bustling with people rushing to and fro. The government of Iraq was brand new, and the foyer of the Council of Ministers looked more like, as my mom would say, "grand central station" ("will you kids get out of my kitchen? It's like Grand Central Station in here!").

A nice-looking Iraqi lady with dark hair cascading around her shoulders sat at an unimpressive metal desk in front of the elevators in the main chamber. She wore a modest, gray dress and white, buttoned shirt with bright red lipstick. I remember being somewhat taken aback by the lack of Muslim garb, but really that was reserved for the rural areas of the country. Here in Baghdad, the women were more cosmopolitan and generally wore Western clothes. Also, it was very common for women to get up in the morning and don the expected Muslim burka to go across the city to work. Once there, they would change into Western attire and put on their makeup. Then at the end of the day, they would wash the makeup off and change back into the head-to-toe black coverings to travel back home.

My translator explained who we were and where we were going. I don't speak Arabic, but I had learned enough words by then halfway through my second tour that even though I couldn't tell you word for word what was being said, I could usually tell you what they were talking about. The bureaucrat nodded in understanding, and we stood there looking back at her. A few confusing and awkward moments passed with no one saying anything. Then, it dawned on us what she was waiting for. She was the gatekeeper to the ministers. If we wanted to get past the gatekeeper and make it to our appointment, she expected us to slip her some money. That was the system. "Want to get upstairs? Pay me."

Well, first, I'm an American. I'm not succumbing to some petty bureaucrat's expectation for a bribe. Second, I had an M4 assault rifle slung over my shoulder and my Beretta M9 9mm pistol on my hip. I am still not succumbing to some petty bureaucrat's expectation for a bribe.

I looked back at my advisor, who by now was looking at me, and I simply said, "Where are the stairs?" We completely ignored the gatekeeper and made our way up the stairs. That was the first time I had run into petty dictator politics firsthand. It wouldn't be the last. See, as the government expands, the worth of the individual shrinks. Big governments—not in terms of number of employees, necessarily, but in the scope of control over the lives of the citizens—are expensive. They suck the wealth right out of the country. And as with a vacuum in a swimming pool, the wealth at the bottom of the pool gets sucked up first. Then, as in I saw repeatedly in Baghdad, too, anyone with a commodity to sell, whether it is black-market gasoline or access to a minister, will sell it. Corruption is everywhere. That's another by-product of powerful government and a people with no value.

The state uses fear to intimidate and subdue the people. In every instance of tyranny, an internal police force is created to keep the people from rising up against the rulers. Remember the Nazis' gestapo and the Soviet Union's KGB? All tyrants and dictators must turn the power of the state against their own people. Fear and intimidation make the people feel isolated, alone, and afraid to speak out. People disappear. Dissenters are sent off to concentration camps, the Gulag, or the killing fields.

As Thomas Jefferson said, "When the people fear their government, there is tyranny; when the government fears the people, there is liberty."

I've seen this in action. Patrolling Baghdad one day with the Iraqi police, we stopped the convoy to survey a site for a future roadblock. The national elections were coming up and we were emplacing roadblocks around the city in an effort to keep out car bombs. It was a typical summer day in Iraq, and that means it felt like it was about six thousand degrees outside. There just so happened to be an enterprising teenager with a little ice cooler welded onto a cart selling cold sodas on the street nearby. "Outstanding!" I thought. Cold drinks were a rare commodity, so I wasn't going to miss this chance.

The kid had a little pushcart with an umbrella duct taped to a broom handle latched to the side of his silver metal cooler to provide just a touch of shade from the scorching sun. Necessity is the mother of invention. It wasn't pretty, but it worked. He picked a great spot. It was a bustling intersection where Al Imam Ali Street, the main north/south thoroughfare in eastern Baghdad, crossed over the Tigris River in the northeast corner of the city.

I found that the average Iraqi was very friendly. This kid was no exception. All smiles and "Hey, mister" as I approached, he genuinely seemed happy to see me. Of course usually Americans mean money, so that probably explained most of his mood. He was wearing a red T-shirt with some American slogan on it, blue jeans with the knees ripped that hung off his skinny frame, and worn-out flip flops on his filthy feet. "Salam Alaikum," I said, giving the traditional Arabic greeting. "Alaikum Salam," he responded, but with a high five thrown in to show how cool he was. I held up a finger to mean one drink "Pepsi," and, grinning, he dove into the cooler, his arms buried to the elbows in ice water. When he came up, his entire demeanor changed.

He looked at me as though the zombie apocalypse was unfolding right over my shoulder. Confused, I wiggled my fingers underneath my body armor and into my pocket to pull out a couple of crumpled and sweaty dollar bills. When I reached out to give them to him, he just shook his head side to side, and with his arms hanging loosely at his side, he stepped back away from me. Again I tried to pay him but received the same response; he just shook his head. Now, instead of being friendly, he suddenly reminded me of a dog who has learned that it is about to get kicked. Head down, not making eye contact with me, he was just afraid. I followed his gaze over my shoulder, and turning, I saw what he was afraid of. There, probably thirty feet behind me, stood two uniformed Iraqi policemen from my convoy, arms crossed over their chests and eyes fixed on the young street vendor. It was as if they were just daring him to take my money.

The kid knew that he might face a good stomping—or in Saddam's day, disappear in the desert—from the police if he dared to accept money from me for the cola. I knew the police wouldn't try anything in my presence, but they just might circle back around later and find this guy. Reluctantly, I turned with the already-opened can and started walking back to the car. I was watching the policemen the whole time. As soon as they turned, too, I let two dollars slip from my hand and onto the ground. Turning, I made sure the kid saw where the money went so he could retrieve it once the police convoy was safely out of sight. That's what it's like living in a police state dominated by fear. A kid selling soda on the street just knows that the uniformed thugs take what they want—no charge.

That's just a small example, but when even a kid selling drinks on the side of the road is inherently intimidated by the state, it shows just how deep this oppression runs. It becomes part of the national character and a way of life, just as intended.

The flip side of this, but still of the same coin, is the sudden narrative of police abuse against the citizens across our country, especially in minority communities. This has been perpetuated from our White House through to the cultural Marxist activists to our streets. I've already mentioned the Black Lives Matter movement. That is a direct result of the new national narrative.

The issue that this administration and its minions—such as the Al Sharptons and others, in what once was a legitimate and honorable civil rights movement—are promoting, namely "a police war on blacks," isn't the real issue. That issue is being promulgated only because it supports their narrative and agenda of control. In this case, this false war works on four fronts. First, it perpetuates the greater feeling of helplessness and disenfranchisement among the minority community. Second, it sows the seeds of mistrust of the figures of authority, our policemen and policewomen. Third, it pits race against race, as the cultural narrative isn't just that it is the police but that it is specifically white police who are at war with the black community. Finally, and this is the real end game of it all, it opens the door to greater control of our local community and state police by the centralized government.

This false narrative is being disseminated from the highest office of our government. The roots of this narrative date back to the beginning of the Obama administration. On July 16, 2009, just seven months after President Obama took office, his friend, Professor Henry Louis Gates, was arrested for disorderly conduct at his Cambridge, Massachusetts, home. The professor came home and found the front door of his house jammed, so he tried to force it open. A neighbor saw him and called 911, thinking she saw someone breaking into a house. Police responded, and the professor, after proving it was in fact his house, pitched such a screaming fit at the police that he got himself arrested.

Five days later, the president was at a press conference and was asked about his friend's arrest. He said this:

> I don't know, not having been there and not seeing all the facts, what role race played in that. But I think it's fair to say, number one, any of us would be pretty angry; number two, that the Cambridge police acted stupidly in arresting somebody when there was already proof that they were in their own home, and, number three, what I think we know separate and apart from this incident is that there's a long history in this country of African Americans and Latinos being stopped by law enforcement disproportionately. (3)

So, in essence, "I don't know the facts, but the police acted stupidly." Statements like that by our chief executive set a precedent. The assumption was that it was the police's fault, and not only was it a mistake, but it was stupid. In addition, Professor Gates was forced to endure this because of institutional racism by the police.

Then on the night of February 26, 2012, there was a shooting in Florida, and an unarmed young black man was dead. Immediately the narrative was that a white, armed, out-of-control wanna-be neighborhood watch hero murdered an unarmed black youth. The problem was, the shooter wasn't white. When it came out that he was actually Hispanic, the news started calling Zimmerman "white Hispanic."

*NBC News* went as far as to edit the recording of the 911 call to make the shooter, George Zimmerman, sound racist. *ABC News*, which had acquired a surveillance tape of Zimmerman walking into the police station, digitally altered the video to cover up the wounds he had on the back of his head after his altercation with the deceased, Treyvon Martin. Thousands of people marched in protest.

The president unleashed the justice department in the town of Sanford, Florida, to conduct a full investigation. Despite all of this, Zimmerman was acquitted of all wrongdoing in the case.

That still wasn't enough to stop our president from turning this into a race issue. Here are his remarks, verbatim, on the case he delivered at a press conference July 19, 2013, more than a full year after the shooting:

> You know, when Trayvon Martin was first shot, I said that this could have been my son. Another way of saying that is Trayvon Martin could have been me thirty-five years ago. And when you think about why, in the African American community at least, there's a lot of pain around what happened here, I think it's important to recognize that the African American community is looking at this issue through a set of experiences and a history that doesn't go away.
>
> There are very few African American men in this country who haven't had the experience of being followed when they were

> shopping in a department store. That includes me. There are very few African American men who haven't had the experience of walking across the street and hearing the locks click on the doors of cars. That happens to me—at least before I was a senator. There are very few African Americans who haven't had the experience of getting on an elevator and a woman clutching her purse nervously and holding her breath until she had a chance to get off. That happens often.
>
> And I don't want to exaggerate this, but those sets of experiences inform how the African American community interprets what happened one night in Florida. And it's inescapable for people to bring those experiences to bear. The African American community is also knowledgeable that there is a history of racial disparities in the application of our criminal laws—everything from the death penalty to enforcement of our drug laws. And that ends up having an impact in terms of how people interpret the case. (4)

His remarks and the agenda they support fall perfectly into the cultural Marxist playbook. The people are divided into groups and pitted against each other so as to minimize the power of any one group. Minimize the power and authority of the local police, concentrating all power in the federal government. Also, the actions of the victim can only be judged as right or wrong if we take into account his historical experiences. There is no objective truth. There is no objective right, wrong, or morality. Everything can be excused and explained once taken in the context of that person's race and life experiences. It all fits so nicely into the cultural Marxists' agenda.

Other such cases followed. When a white police officer shot and killed Michael Brown, another unarmed black man in Ferguson, Missouri, the federal justice department once again launched a full investigation. The short story of the case is that a guy robbed a convenience store, assaulting the store owner in the process. The store owner called 911. There was a police officer a very short distance away, and he responded. The alleged perpetrator attacked the police officer while the officer was still in his car and, punching him several times in the face, tried to take the policeman's gun. Failing that, the perpetrator ran away from the car. The policeman called for the guy to stop. He didn't. Instead, Michael Brown turned and once again ran at the officer. They had already been in a fist fight. Brown had already tried to take his gun. So when Brown repeatedly ignored the officer's call to freeze and get down and continued to charge him, the officer fired.

The president sent three White House representatives to the Brown funeral. The city of Ferguson burned as riots tore through the city. All the forensic evidence, eyewitness reports, and the officer's own testimony indicated that the officer's act was in self-defense. None of that mattered.

As Barack Obama stated in his 1995 book, *Dreams of My Father*, "Once I found an issue enough people cared about, I could take them into action. With enough actions, I could start to build power. Issues, actions, power, self-interest. I liked these concepts. They bespoke a certain hardheadedness, a worldly lack of sentiment; politics, not religion." (5)

The issues at work here were racist cops killing unarmed black men and the general disenfranchisement of the minority community. It doesn't matter if there is any truth to the narrative. The narrative itself is all that is important. As for the federal government taking control of our local police forces, Obama said, "We have a great opportunity ... to really transform how we think about community law enforcement relations." That means control from one central authority in Washington.

The more powerful we allow government to become, the less value is left for us. Of course, that means less freedom too. Rights are gone. You can't have a state that is omnipotent in everyone's life and still allow those people to complain. No freedom of speech. You can't have an all-powerful government that can drag people out of their house in the middle of the night and still allow them to have firearms. No right to bear arms. You can't have an all-powerful government that will kick you out of your home or seize your business with no notice and no hearing and still allow them private property rights. That is why in such a tyrannical system, free market capitalism cannot exist either.

And that goes a long way toward explaining why all these potentate countries run by dictators are poor. It can happen here too. The Marxists will claim that they can save us. They will claim that the answer lies in granting the central power more and more authority. Enemies will be declared the root of all our problems, whether these are Christians, "the rich," those tea party extremists, or racist police.

But there is a problem with their narrative. You see, no other economic system has brought more people out of poverty, provided for the health and well-being of millions, and raised the standard of living in more societies than capitalism. When people cooperate to fulfill their own self-interest, they all benefit.

Capitalism and freedom are inextricably linked. When the Declaration of Independence was first drafted, it read, "We hold these truths to be self-evident, that all men are created equal and endowed by their Creator with certain unalienable Rights, that among these are life, liberty, and property."

The word "property" was changed later to read "pursuit of happiness" because the founders did not want the document to be perceived as supporting slavery. But the first draft read "property." Why?

Maybe Frédéric Bastiat said it a bit better back in 1850 in *The Law*. "Life, faculties, production—in other words individuality, liberty, property—that is man. And in spite of the cunning of artful political leaders, these three gifts from God precede all human legislation, and are superior to it." (6)

The concept of property and private property rights is indispensable to freedom and liberty—as well as to capitalism. Realize first that the term property includes much more than the material items we buy, store, or make. Property also includes our thoughts, beliefs, values, convictions, actions, education and experience, and labor. Our voices, spirituality, and even our lives are also our property. What we do with our property, how we employ it to improve our lives and take care of our families, ought to be completely up to us. Government was created, and its only function should be, to protect our property and our right to employ or not employ them as we see fit.

The Declaration of Independence listed those three specific rights, and then the very next line explained the function of government: "That to secure these rights, Governments are instituted among Men." Then, in the US Constitution, the government created specifically to secure our rights is strictly limited in its power, lest the government created by the governed become too powerful. Also, to further restrict the power of government and to secure our rights and property, the Bill of Rights was added to the Constitution before the states would ratify it.

So our God-given rights are also our property, government exists to secure these rights, and the Constitution exists to protect us from government. The freedom assured to the people in such an arrangement naturally leads to capitalism. It is this system, a federal government with strictly limited powers and a populace with the freedom to employ their property as they wish that allowed the United States to rise from its existence as a small, backward agrarian society to becoming a world power in less than a century.

It is this legal respect for personal property that allowed great innovation, invention, and industry to flourish. It is the mobility that was granted to our people by our freedoms that allowed the country to grow and our people to prosper. The extension of the concept of property to include our ideas allowed the Wright Brothers to invent the first powered aircraft. It allowed the Thomas Edisons, Henry Fords, and the Steve Jobs of our country to patent and protect their ideas, grow companies, and provide incomes and livelihoods to untold millions of people.

I've seen the other side. In my time in the Army, I've served both in Germany and in South Korea. I've seen what communism looks like staring back from across Europe's Iron Curtain and the Demilitarized Zone. I've seen the misery and poverty that comes from a centrally planned economy where personal property rights don't exist and liberty is unknown. The walls that I guarded wearing the uniform of freedom were not constructed by us to keep the forces of communism out. Those walls were built by the forces of communism to hold their own people in.

For once you strip the people of their liberty, their freedom, and their property in all its forms, you've stripped them of their individuality. They no longer exist for themselves; they no longer have any worth except to fill some role that benefits the state. They are similar to workers in an anthill, with no individual rights, no personal property, and no way to improve their lives, because all property and all means of production belong to the queen.

But now, our Constitution and the concept of property are under attack. We have a president who is alienating those who create. He and his allies on the Left are making enemies of those who innovate, build, and dream. He is espousing a philosophy that states that for anyone to get ahead, we have to pull the successful among us down. Somehow he is trying to convince us that by taking money from some of our citizens and giving that money to the government, the poor among us will be better off. The truth is, all that will happen is that all of us become poorer.

This rhetoric is designed to simultaneously group us into the masses and divide us into economic groups. It has been called class warfare, but it goes much deeper. The term "fairness" is used over and over to espouse a false argument that there should be equality in outcome, that we should all be the same, that some having more is somehow unfair to those who have less. In capitalism, wealth can be created exponentially through innovation, invention, and starting a small business—and then hiring people and becoming a large business. Having wealth and creating wealth is not dependent on seizing the wealth from others. Now we are being told that we can achieve equality and fairness only by seizing the wealth of others, giving it to those who do not contribute.

We must recognize that if we stand idly by and, through our inaction, allow the government to seize the property of some of our citizens under the false premise that it benefits us all, we all lose. For once a freedom is lost, once we surrender a liberty, it will not come back. We must recognize that the government is trying to convince us that it is only seeking to achieve fairness and that only it can best determine what that means—and it will take, by force, the property from some of our citizens for those ends. How is it, to paraphrase the words of Mark Levine, that we are wise enough to choose our leaders but not our lightbulbs? This entire concept turns our founding on its head, and the government becomes supreme. The people have surrendered their liberty.

Capitalism, and the concept of private property, has proven that one can employ his or her property, including the ideas, labor, capital, experience, education, hard work, spirituality, time, and dreams, putting them to work to advance his or her well-being, raise a family, and leave this a better country.

This also means we leave this a better world for our children than how we inherited it. We are close to losing this America. We are close to losing our freedoms. We now have a government that does not respect personal property and believes it can choose better how we should employ our property. For every new power the government gains, it must necessarily take a similar amount of freedom from us.

Unlike wealth and prosperity, liberty is a zero-sum game.

But wait, there's more! If you peel back the onion skin one more time, there is still a deeper reason for this respect for private property at our founding. At its heart lies the philosophy of the supremacy of God's law and where our rights come from and why.

*Fox News* conducted a survey on July 4, 2015, Independence Day, asking people, "What makes America great?" or, "Why are you proud to be an American?" Typical answers were, "Opportunity to succeed," aka the American Dream, or "Freedom of speech," but they are missing the most fundamental point of what set America apart, which is far more profound.

In summer 2005, I was working the streets of Baghdad as an intelligence officer. Of the many local groups that I had contacts with was the Iraqi staff of an American contracting company that translated newspapers, radio broadcasts, and television reports from all around the Middle East into English. The idea was that we would then know what the Iraqis were saying about us and the American operations in general. Every Wednesday, I made my way down to their offices in the green zone, and we held a round table where we discussed the latest "word on the streets." This meant they would bring with them rumors and the general scuttlebutt from their neighborhoods. This was of particular interest while American forces were conducting counterinsurgency operations in and around the city of six million people. That was about the only feedback we got on how we were doing in winning over the people's hearts and minds.

On one particularly hot Wednesday round table, I was asked, "What is American democracy?" and "What is freedom?" They were asking this as the worst sectarian violence of the war so far was tearing their capital city apart. To the Iraqis, most of whom had never known anything but total dictatorship under Saddam, the conception of freedom was synonymous with anarchy. They had no history of being a free people and didn't know what that meant at all. To some, it meant you were absolutely free of any consequences. If you wanted to shoot your neighbor in the head, no problem. You were free. Go shoot him in the head. Others were already longing for the return of a government such as what they had under Saddam Hussein. Yes, he was a tyrant, but there was order. The people had lived in constant fear of being suspected as enemies of the state, and such an accusation could lead to imprisonment, torture, or death, being dragged out into the desert and getting a bullet in the head. But under Saddam there were no car bombs, no IEDs, no drive-by shootings, and no mafia turf wars. All of that and more had become part of the everyday existence in Iraq during the war.

These people who were genuinely worried about getting home alive really wanted to know what freedom meant to an American. I could feel the sweat drip down my back as I pondered what to say. The easy answer to their question would have been, "In America, the people vote for our leaders." But there is so much more.

The true significance of America's founding was that here we acknowledge and enshrine the basic worth and dignity of the individual citizen. By acknowledging that we, the people, derive our value and therefore our rights from our Creator, and those cannot be given or taken by any government or sovereign, this country establishes the conditions for everything else—a constitutionally limited government, the Bill of Rights, a strong and thriving free-market system, respect for private property and contracts, and an unbiased judicial system.

Our system of government based on God-given rights automatically means equality and tolerance. We are all created in God's image. The poorest and the richest among us possess the exact same value, the exact same rights, and, in theory, the exact same amount of political power. The poorest and the richest among us, according to our founding principles, are equals before the law, and no one is above the law. No one has the inherent right to rule over us. That includes temporary officials—elected, appointed, or otherwise. We are all equal in the eyes of God and therefore are all equal under the rule of law.

Also, as our founders recognized, government exists at the consent of the governed and only to protect our rights. America is a great country. It was the principles of our founding that were based on God's law and nature's law that made us so.

Those unique factors are what make America special. That is why America rose from a backward collection of agrarian colonies to become the world's preeminent superpower in 150 years. No other government in the history of mankind had been founded on such principles. That is why America is exceptional. The first settlers to this land came here to find religious liberty. This country was founded on Judeo-Christian values. America has been a beacon of freedom throughout the world since our founding.

Whether we remain this beacon of freedom is yet to be seen; without a doubt, it is slipping away at an alarming rate.

It is no coincidence that as the country turns from our traditions, history, and values, our government becomes more tyrannical. Our founders thought it could happen. John Adams warned, "Avarice, ambition, revenge and licentiousness would break the strongest cords of our Constitution. Our Constitution was made only for a moral and religious people. It is wholly inadequate to the government of any other." (7)

The frailty of our freedoms were not lost to future generations. In 1922 the Reverend William T. Rogers felt it important to include a warning to his congregation in his 4th of July newsletter of the First Presbyterian Church, Macomb Illinois, called the The Harold and Presbyter. It was the 146th anniversary of the Declaration of Independence. As he and his church celebrated America's founding, Reverend Rogers reminded his readers of our country's special roots. "A nation's character is largely determined by its pioneers. Its first laws give direction to its later legislation" he rightly observed. The good reverend also observed the nature and character of America and how it could all slip away. "God's hand is clearly seen in the early settlement of the New World. In celebrating our independence, it would be well to recall that the Scriptures molded these people, and unless it continues to guide our nation liberty will perish."(8)

As those patriots who signed the Declaration of Independence declared, "With a firm reliance on the protection of divine Providence, we mutually pledge to each other our Lives, our Fortunes, and our Sacred Honor." To me, you can't believe in God and not believe in freedom. You can't simultaneously believe you should love your neighbors as yourself and still somehow believe you have the right to rule over them.

Explaining those principles to novices to any kind of representative form of government was hard. They had never known any kind of life in which the average person had no intrinsic value whatsoever other than to serve the state. I generally got the deer-in-the-headlights stare back at me as they tried to compute that every citizen has worth and that the government is subordinate to the people.

I remember wondering then what it must be like to live like that, to be in a country right at the turning point between freedom and tyranny. These people in front of me, for the first time ever had the real possibility to seize freedom from despotism. To me at the time, America was still free. I hate using past tense in that sentence. But I felt that America still stood for something. I think America is at that same tipping point where we could plunge into tyranny or remain a free republic. Maybe we've already passed it. I sincerely hope not.

Two years earlier, I was a company commander leading my soldiers into Iraq during the invasion in 2003. I gathered my young soldiers the night before we were to leave the staging camp in Kuwait to begin our drive into Iraq. I knew they were nervous and had no idea what to expect once they crossed that line, going into harm's way for the first time. It was to be my first time too. But as their commander, It was my job to bolster their spirits and as best I could, calm their fears.

Borrowing from Colonel Joshua Chamberlain's speech to the Maine deserters on the eve of the Battle of Gettysburg, I told them what I thought it meant to wear the uniform of an American soldier. Paraphrasing now, I told them that throughout history, the approach of a foreign army into one's land has always meant slaughter, enslavement, looting, rape, and pillaging, except when it was an American soldier who is coming. Then it has always meant liberation. We were just in our cause and were on the march to set another people free from tyranny. Despite reports you might see now, in 2003 we were welcomed by the Iraqi people as liberators.

In America we have had the privilege of living in a "free" country. We have never felt the chains of a dictatorship around our necks. I have always considered myself very lucky to have been born here. But at the same time, having never known tyranny, will we recognize only too late that our country has fundamentally transformed from a representative, constitutional republic to a socialist oligarchy or worse? No tyrant could successfully make that transformation in America without first stamping God out of His central position in our lives and culture.

Would we even recognize it as the transformation began and carried out its course? Even after fighting wars throughout the last century to defeat or contain just this sort of tyranny, would we know when it came here? Certainly it wouldn't come from a conquering army from without but rather through a steady erosion of all of our founding principles from within. It would be the death of a thousand cuts, some deeper and swifter than others but all with the same goal, to bleed us of our liberty.

On April 3, 1965, radio commentary legend Paul Harvey issued a warning to America. Titled "If I were the Devil," it was a warning to America. His broadcast was over fifty years ago, and it turned out to be spot-on.

Paul Harvey's warning came at a time of upheaval in America. The baby boomer generation was now in college, and there were widespread revolts and riots across the country. The cultural Marxism campaign had had two full generations in which to go to work in our institutions, and the effects were beginning to show. A strong antiestablishment, anti-American mentality was starting to take hold, especially in our universities.

I firmly believe that God's hand was over our founding fathers. The nation they created, especially in a time of kings, queens, and empires, was amazing in its simplicity. The original Constitution was six pages long. Add the Bill of Rights, and we're at ten pages. I am convinced that the creation of a government subordinate to a citizenry who is always assumed to be a free people and with rights guaranteed to them by limiting that government so succinctly could not have happened without guidance from above.

> **1 Peter 2:9** But you are a chosen people, a royal priesthood, a holy nation, God's special possession, that you may declare the praises of him who called you out of darkness into his wonderful light.

This country they created not only protected the freedom of its own citizens but since has also become a beacon of freedom for the entire world. Through our sweat, treasure, and blood, driven by these founding virtues, we spread that liberty to countless millions in foreign lands as well.

Would it, then, be a big surprise if America were the "ripest apple on the tree" for the enemy to take down and destroy? For if America, with its limited government that is "of the people, by the people, for the people" and guarantees personal liberty with firm roots in Christian-Judeo traditions, is guided by God, then it stands to reason that those who push for an all-powerful government that seeks to enslave its people and spread darkness across the world would be driven by the enemy.

Because it is just so spot-on in its prophetic message, I am going to include the entire text of Paul Harvey's warning to America. As you read this, remember that is was written and first broadcast in 1965. It could have very well been written yesterday.

"If I Were the Devil"

> If I were the Prince of Darkness I would want to engulf the whole earth in darkness.
>
> I'd have a third of its real estate and four-fifths of its population, but I would not be happy until I had seized the ripest apple on the tree.
>
> So I should set about however necessary, to take over the United States.

I would begin with a campaign of whispers.

With the wisdom of a serpent, I would whispers to you as I whispered to Eve, "Do as you please."

To the young I would whisper, "The Bible is a myth." I would convince them that "man created God," instead of the other way around. I would confide that "what is bad is good and what is good is square."

In the ears of the young married, I would whisper that work is debasing, that cocktail parties are good for you. I would caution them not to be "extreme" in religion, in patriotism, in moral conduct.

And the old I would teach to pray—to say after me—"Our father which art in Washington."

Then I'd get organized.

I'd educate authors in how to make lurid literature exciting so that anything else would appear dull, uninteresting.

I'd threaten TV with dirtier movies, and vice-versa.

I'd infiltrate unions and urge more loafing, less work. Idle hands usually work for me.

I'd peddle narcotics to whom I could, I'd sell alcohol to ladies and gentlemen of distinction, I'd tranquilize the rest with pills.

If I were the Devil, I would encourage schools to refine young intellects, but neglect to discipline emotions; let those run wild.

I'd designate an atheist to front for me before the highest courts, and I'd get preachers to say, "She's right."

With flattery and promises of power, I would get the courts to vote against God and in favor of pornography.

Thus I would evict God from the courthouse, then from the schoolhouse, then from the Houses of Congress.

Then in his own churches, I'd substitute psychology for religion and deify science.

If I were Satan, I'd make the symbol of Easter an egg and the symbol of Christmas a bottle.

> If I were the Devil, I'd take from those who have and give to those who wanted until I had killed the incentive of the ambitious. Then my police state would force everybody back to work.
>
> Then I would separate families, putting children in uniform, women in coal mines, and objectors in slave-labor camps.
>
> If I were Satan, I'd just keep doing what I'm doing, and the whole world would go to hell as sure as the Devil. (9)

Those whispers that Paul Harvey mentioned in 1965 have risen to a crescendo now. Everything that was once just part of our national character is being attacked. Traditional marriage, prayer, the sanctity of the lives of unborn babies, the respect for our police, and basic morality are all targets. The basic narrative being preached in our schools, the TV news and talk shows, the press, our courts, and the halls of government is that if you stand on the values that once made this country the most advanced and the freest in the world, then you are the problem.

Michael Walsh examines another aspect of this in *The Devil's Pleasure Palace: The Cult of Critical Theory and the Subversion of the West*:

> The attack on normative heterosexuality ... invariably disguised as a movement for "rights"...is fundamental to the success of Critical Theory ... If a wedge could be driven between men and women, if the nuclear family could be cracked, if women could be convinced to fear and hate men...then that political party that had adopted Critical Theory could make single women one of their strongest voting blocs....
>
> The result has been entirely predictable: masculinized women, feminized men, falling rates of childbirth in the Western world, and the creation of a technocratic political class that can type but do little real work in the traditional sense. Coeducational college campuses have quickly mutated from sexually segregated living quarters to coed dorms to

> the "hookup culture"... to a newly puritanical and explicitly anti-male "rape culture" hysteria, in which sexual commissars promulgate step-by-step rules for sexual encounters and often dispense completely with due process when adjudicating complaints from female students.
>
> With the collapse of the Soviet Union, our campuses now represent the largest concentration of Marxist dogma in the world. The irrational adolescent outbursts of the 1960s have become institutionalized into a "permanent revolution." Our professors glance over their shoulders, hoping the current mode will blow over before a student's denunciation obliterates a life's work; some audio-tape their lectures, fearing accusations of "insensitivity" by some enraged "Red Guard." Students at the University of Virginia recently petitioned successfully to drop the requirement to read Homer, Chaucer, and other DEMS (Dead European Males) because such writings are considered ethnocentric, phallocentric, and generally inferior to the "more relevant" third-world, female, or homosexual authors.
>
> —"Frankfurt School and Political Correctness," Michael Minnicino (10).

One of the key founders of the Frankfurt School was Georg Lukacs. His book, *History and Class Consciousness*, was a primary driving force of the philosophy of the Frankfurt School and the cultural Marxist movement that followed. Lukacs also served as the cultural minister of Hungary. In Hungary, his orders mandating sex education in the schools, easy access to contraception, and the loosening of divorce laws were all intended to weaken the institution of marriage. Weakening the institution of marriage would in turn weaken families. The ultimate goal was to disconnect children from their parents. Then, with control of the schools from kindergarten to PhDs, kids with no roots and loose holds on their heritage and identities would be ripe for indoctrination. That was and still is their true intention.

Truth is the death of intention.

—Walter Benjamin, The Frankfurt School.

The eroticism of the counterculture meant much more than free love and a violent attack on the nuclear family. It also meant the legitimization of philosophical *eros.* People were trained to see themselves as objects, determined by their "natures." The importance of the individual as a person gifted with the divine spark of creativity, capable of acting upon all human civilization, was replaced by the idea that the person is important because he or she is black, or a woman, or feels homosexual impulses. This explains the deformation of the civil rights movement into a "black power" movement, and the transformation of the legitimate issue of civil rights for women into feminism. Discussion of women's civil rights was forced into being just another "liberation cult," complete with bra-burning and other, sometimes openly Astarte-style, rituals; a review of Kate Millet's *Sexual Politics* (1970) and Germaine Greer's *The Female Eunuch* (1971) reveals complete reliance on Marcuse, Fromm, Reich, and other Freudian extremists.

We have to keep in mind that the process of indoctrination is not the end game. The process of indoctrination is only important because once the citizens' way of life is destroyed, the citizens' natural instincts will be to grasp onto something else, something that will bring order back out of chaos, just like some of the Iraqis in 2005 were longing for the order, if not the man, of Saddam Hussein. It is the intent of the cultural Marxist that full government control and power be the only remaining option for obtaining that "something else."

If you think this view is a bit extreme, think of the modern cultural Marxist's bible, Saul Alinsky's *Rules for Radicals.* If what our country once stood for was good and decent and was guided by God's hand, then what is guiding the forces that seek to destroy it? Alinsky's 1971 book includes a dedication: "Lest we forget at least an over-the-shoulder acknowledgment to the very first radical: from all our legends, mythology, and history … the first radical known to man who rebelled against the establishment and did it so effectively that he at least won his own kingdom—Lucifer." (11)

# 4

## Life

**"God's love does not distinguish between the infant in the mother's womb or the child or the youth or the adult or the older person. In each one God sees His image and likeness. Human life is a manifestation of God and His glory."**

**— Pope Benedict XVI**

Do you believe in ghosts? Hang in there, I'm going somewhere with this. Apparently, millions of Americans do believe in ghosts of some kind. There are no less than thirty-seven ghost and paranormal cable and network shows on television right now. A 2013 *Huffington Post* poll shows that 45 percent of Americans believe in ghosts or that the spirits of dead people can come back in certain places and situations.

This may seem like an outrageous comparison and analogy, but bear with me. Just what is a ghost? The poll vaguely defined it as life after death or spirits. If a ghost is in fact a spirit of a once-living person, then it stands to reason that this spirit existed within the body of the living person during his or her mortal life. But this spirit must be separate and distinct from the mortal body to transcend this life and become a ghost in the afterlife. It is also assumed to be immortal.

Another accepted definition of this disembodied spirit is "soul." According to Dictionary.com, "soul" is defined as "the spiritual part of humans regarded in its moral aspect, or as believed to survive death and be subject to happiness or misery in a life to come." Whether a spirit hanging around an old movie theater or your basement is experiencing happiness or misery would be left to the ghost to decide. But we can exchange the word "ghost" for the word "soul" and still be referring to the same disembodied spirit.

For argument's sake, we can make the mental leap to state that human beings have souls. If that is true, where did these come from? Why is it that we don't say horse beings or dog beings and instead reserve that term for ourselves, human beings? The difference lies in the fact that, as we are told in Genesis chapter 5, verse 1, "In the day God created man, He made him in the likeness of God."

I know that starting a discussion about ghosts to confirm the existence of souls within our corporal bodies may be a stretch. But it seems more and more that Americans are in denial of the existence of a life beyond the one here on terra firma. It is unfortunate that millions of folks watch shows about zombies or the apocalyptic end of the world or of a haunted house but still deny the existence of their own immortal soul. So there seems to be a draw to entertainment that depicts a life after the death of our bodies; if that exists, what is it that lives on? The soul, of course. God's presence in our bodies.

> **Ezekiel 18:4** Behold, all souls are mine; the soul of the father as well as the soul of the son is mine.

When does that happen? When does God impart the immortal soul into the mortal body of a person?

The conception and birth of a human baby is still a spiritual event for me. I love babies, all babies, and I always have. They represent pure innocence.

Little defenseless babies are all giggles and cries. They also represent God's purpose in this life. Everything about them is magical and special. A baby represents the hope that still exists in this world. A baby can grow up to be anything. He or she might cure cancer or be the next Rembrandt. Who knows? The sky's the limit.

> **Luke 18:16** But Jesus called them *unto him*, and said, "Suffer little children to come unto me, and forbid them not: for of such is the kingdom of God."

From a tiny cluster of cells to a bouncing baby, fetal development is an amazing process. At one month, your baby is an embryo consisting of two layers of cells from which all her organs and body parts will develop. In the second month she is now about the size of a kidney bean and is constantly moving. She has distinct, slightly webbed fingers. By the end of the first trimester, the baby is about three inches long and weighs nearly an ounce. Her tiny, unique fingerprints are now in place.

At four months, your baby is now about five inches long and weighs five ounces. His skeleton is starting to harden from rubbery cartilage to bone. Eyebrows and eyelids are in place in the fifth month. Your baby would now be more than ten inches long if you stretched out his legs. As the second trimester closes, your baby weighs about a pound and a half. His wrinkled skin is starting to smooth out as he puts on baby fat.

At seven months, your baby is more than fifteen inches long. She can open and close her eyes and follow a light. Your baby now weighs about four and three-quarter pounds. Her layers of fat are filling her out, making her rounder, and her lungs are well developed. Babies vary widely in size at this stage, just before the baby takes her first breath of air.

The stages of a baby's development have been recorded, studied, filmed, and analyzed from conception through birth, but there is one question that cannot be solved by any instrument. Expectant moms and dads watch their babies grow on sonograms and watch as little arms and legs move inside Mommy's belly. At around sixteen weeks or so, you can find out if you're having a boy or a girl—but don't; that would spoil the surprise! I've had four kids, and never once did I want to know the sex of the baby before its birthday. I like surprises. Three boys and a girl.

What you can't see is when that little growing life is imbued by God with his soul. No doctor on earth can show you one frame of a developing baby and say, "This embryo still has no soul," and then show you another picture taken the next day and say, "Hey, look! God graced your baby with a soul last night."

Medical science, despite all of its advances, cannot know whether a baby receives his soul at conception, in the first trimester, or at the father's snipping of the umbilical cord. Thus, who can guess when it would be ok to kill the baby? If each of us, and every baby, is made in the likeness of God, then from where would we derive the authority to end that little life? The answer is, we don't have any such authority, and that is all part of a larger problem. Our society has abolished religion and decreed that belief in God, particularly Christian belief, is a tiresome, outmoded way of thinking and that science should reign supreme. Why indeed should a secular society quibble about what is done with dead people who have no right to life? Once it's been decided that the babies are of no value, it's a hop, skip, and a jump to deciding that their parts can be sold without guilt. The sad irony, of course, is that this mentality is coming to the fore just at the time that science is able to show us the baby in the womb and keep premature babies alive at earlier and earlier stages of development.

I believe that at that exact magical moment when God endows the yet unborn baby with a soul, He also endows her with rights. The first of these, of course, is the right to life. This sanctity of human life was acknowledged by our founders as preeminent among our God-given rights.

> **Leviticus 24:17–18** Whoever takes a human life shall surely be put to death.

I don't think it was a coincidence that when Thomas Jefferson listed our inalienable rights in the Declaration of Independence, life was first. Not only does everything else, of course, rely on our being alive, but his statement also means no one can take our lives.

> Each man is equally entitled to his life with every other man; each man has an equal title to God-given liberties along with every other.
>
> —Clarence Carson

One would think that this is common sense. Of course all human life is sacred. Of course you can't just go around killing people. You can't. It's against both man's and God's law. But governments do it all the time. People generally don't freely give up their liberty. The imposition of an omnipotent, all-controlling, centralized government always, always has come with mass death. This type of control has to be imposed. Communism is an idea so good it has to be mandatory.

There are so many examples throughout history and across the world that prove this point. The leaders of the revolution always believe they are acting in the interest of the greater good. What guys like Stalin, Mao, Pol Pot, and Hitler don't seem to understand or care about is that people are God's precious creations and therefore automatically free. They don't want to surrender their private property and move onto the collective farm. They don't want to be herded into ghettos and watch their children slowly starve. So Marxism has to be forced onto them. It's for the "greater good," or, in today's language, it occurs in the name of social justice.

When the communists took over Russia, the imposition of Marxism resulted in millions of innocent deaths of Russia's own citizens. In his 1983 book, *Unnatural Deaths in the U.S.S.R.: 1928–1954*, I. G. Dyadkin estimated that the USSR suffered 56–62 million unnatural deaths during that period, with 34–49 million directly linked to then President Josef Stalin. (1) When the national socialists, with Adolf Hitler as the party leader, took power in Germany, in 1933, they also had to impose their new brand of socialism. Hitler's willing executioners in Germany killed up to 12 million, to include not only Jews but also homosexuals, gypsies, Russian POWs, mentally and physically disabled, and the elderly. Anyone who could be deemed an enemy of the state or of the revolution, which it was even if the Nazis didn't call it that, had to be eliminated.

When Mao's communist party took power in China, as he imposed his Great Leap Forward, many millions of his own citizens were destroyed. Estimates are up to 70 million from 1958 to 1962, when the nation faced famine, systematic torture, brutality, starvation, and killing of Chinese peasants—similar to World War II in its magnitude. At least 45 million people were worked, starved, or beaten to death in China.

Usually those most opposed to communism are authority figures such as teachers, priests, industrialists, and landowners. But no one is ever safe. It is the same story every time. Pol Pot in Cambodia killed 1.7 million of his own people, or 25 percent of the entire population. Idi Amin in Uganda killed 300,000. North Korea's turning communist cost the lives of 1.6 million, and the camps there still exist. The communist revolution in our own hemisphere, Cuba, under the Castro brothers with their henchman, Che Guevara, murdered at least 85,675 people.

"The peaceful road is eliminated and violence is inevitable. In order to achieve socialist regimes there will flow rivers of blood," Che explained. "the road to liberation should be continued even if it means the loss of millions of atomic victims." (2) The revolution is all that matters. Without fail, the revolutionary screams for equality and then takes power, crushing all opposition and burying them in mass graves.

How can people do that to their fellow man? In such a system, the state is the only thing that is important. It controls everything—where you live, what you do for a living, what you can buy, what kind of car you can own even what type of lightbulbs you can use in your bathroom. The individual citizen has no intrinsic value. The only worth any one person has consists of his or her ability to serve the state. Those who don't serve the state need to be eliminated. The person has no rights. The person has no worth. The citizens transform from person to people to the masses, becoming less than human. The dehumanization of the individual citizen is a critical aspect of the Marxist and even the cultural Marxist. We lose our identity as individuals. It is much easier to drag people out of their houses in the middle of the night and stuff them into boxcars if they're not really people anyway. As a Nazi genocidal executioner, speaking for all his brethren, stated on the killing of Jews during the Holocaust, "The Jew was not acknowledged by us to be a human being." (3)

But that could never happen here, right? We have rights in America. The value and worth of the individual citizen is enshrined in our national heritage and in our founding, right? Not so fast. Beginning in the late nineteenth century, there was a movement in this country claiming that population control was the best means to improve society. These people were extremely racist. Thinking that certain races were inherently superior and therefore more desirable than others, they sought to curb the reproduction of the less desirable. They sought to contain the "inferior" races through segregation, sterilization, birth control, and abortion. (This, coincidentally—or maybe not so coincidentally—was at the same time that eliminationist anti-Semitism was really taking hold in Germany.) Through these means, the ultimate goal was the elimination of not only inferior races but also the sick, infirm, and mentally handicapped of all races.

In 1922, Margaret Sanger, the founder of Planned Parenthood, wrote her work, *Woman, Morality, and Birth Control*. In it, she addressed the problem of how to get minorities to willingly participate in their own elimination through birth control and abortion. She called her work the "Negro Project." Then, through careful propaganda she set out to recruit leaders from the black community to help her sell her racist ideology of birth control and abortion. Remember, her intent was the elimination of the African-American race. Knowing that American blacks were religious, she thought the best approach was through the churches, where they could reach the widest audience. However, for obvious reasons, she had to keep the true and sinister motives secret. "We should hire three or four colored ministers, preferably with social-service backgrounds and with engaging personalities," she said in a letter concerning the Negro Project. "The most successful educational approach to the Negro is through a religious appeal. We don't want the word to go out that we want to exterminate the Negro population, and the minister is the man who can straighten out that idea if it ever occurs to any of their more rebellious members."(4) The goal was the extermination of the "Negro" population. Planned Parenthood? Yes, they were enlisting the help of the people they wanted dead to get the job done.

Today the private, for-profit Planned Parenthood's abortion clinics are by far most prevalent in minority communities. Abortions themselves are by far more prevalent among minorities, especially African Americans, than they are among whites. All life is not assumed to be precious creations of God. In 1973, if the Supreme Court had considered the cause of murdering babies instead of aborting fetuses, I wonder if the ruling would have been the same. Since then, there have been more than fifty-four million babies murdered through abortion, and that number has disproportionately impacted the black community.

It isn't only abortion. In the late 1960s and 1970s, the domestic terrorist group, the Weather Underground (WU), run by Bill Ayers and his wife, Bernadine Dohrn, had plans to fundamentally transform America into a communist state. They, together with Bill's comrades Mark Rudd, Linda Evans, Jeff Jones, and others, started a splinter group of the Marxist Students for a Democratic Society, calling for a violent Marxist revolution. They really believed that with the help of the Cubans, Chinese, Russians, and North Vietnamese, they could overthrow the American government and impose a communist state here. They knew there were some Americans who would never submit. The plan was to send these diehard, freedom-loving capitalists to reeducation camps, as had been done in other countries following Marxist revolutions. Still, they acknowledged there would be those who would still resist. What was their plan to deal with those people? Larry Grathwohl, then an FBI agent, was able to infiltrate the WU. He was present during numerous strategy meetings where the group's final plans were discussed. In a 1982 interview with the Western Goals Foundation, Grathwohl revealed the WU's plan:

> I asked, "Well what is going to happen to those people we can't reeducate, that are diehard capitalists?" And the reply was that they'd have to be eliminated.
>
> And when I pursued this further, they estimated they would have to eliminate twenty-five million people in these reeducation centers.
>
> And when I say "eliminate," I mean "kill."
>
> Twenty-five million people.
>
> I want you to imagine sitting in a room with twenty-five people, most of which have graduate degrees, from Columbia and other well-known educational centers, and hear them figuring out the logistics for the elimination of twenty-five million people, and they were dead serious. (5)

There is a glimpse inside the mind of the Marxist, cultural Marxist and revolutionary. Ayers summed up the organization's ideology as follows: "Kill all the rich people. Break up their cars and apartments. Bring the revolution home. Kill your parents."

But we Americans could never be dehumanized by our own government, right? Well, recent events, laws, and policies would argue otherwise. Obamacare, for example, is now the law of the land, pushed by the progressive cultural Marxists in Washington and their supporting crony groups such as the AARP. Now the federal government has injected itself into the relationship you had with your family doctor. Common Core, the top-down, one-size-fits-all education system coming from Washington, now rules over your child's teachers, transforming the classroom from a place of actual learning into a fearful place of standardized test scores and teacher evaluations. The EPA rules over a world where the drainage ditch in your yard becomes an inland waterway and Mr. and Mrs. Smith become Case #1133A. Our veterans die by the thousands while waiting for approval for health care and doctor appointments from an all-powerful bureaucracy, where the employees are incentivized not by the number of our veterans who receive care but by the number of "cases" they open and close. So instead of helping one veteran at a time, and I know this from firsthand experience, each veteran is turned into multiple cases to benefit the bureaucrat. People die in the meantime. The federal government funds Planned Parenthood every year with more than $500 million, forcing all of us to contribute to Margaret Sanger's vision of racist murder. That isn't dehumanizing?

This is a dangerous trend that *has* to be reversed. Each one of us is special, created equal in God's own image, endowed by Him with His soul and our rights. We are the supreme masters over any government we ourselves created. We are not serfs to be ruled. We have worth and value beyond that which any mortal man can assign for his own benefit. Those values have to be reflected in our national character and in our policies. We are free because God gave us our right to life. We have the inherent right to abolish any government that no longer serves us. Government never has the power to abolish us because we no longer serve it.

# 5

## ONLY GOD CAN FIX THIS

**"The foundation of national morality must be laid in private families.... How is it possible that Children can have any just Sense of the sacred Obligations of Morality or Religion if, from their earliest Infancy, they learn their Mothers live in habitual Infidelity to their fathers, and their fathers in as constant Infidelity to their Mothers? "**

**— JOHN ADAMS, DIARY, JUNE 2, 1778**

TIMES OF CONFUSION, trouble, despair, turmoil and sorrow hit all of us. Believers in Christ have a well, our faith, to draw strength from to see us through these bad times. My faith sustains me through the bad times and makes me thankful when things are good. My faith has become part of me.

As Psalm 23 states, "The LORD is my shepherd; I shall not want. He maketh me to lie down in green pastures: He leadeth me beside the still waters. He restoreth my soul: he leadeth me in the paths of righteousness for His name's sake. Yea, though I walk through the valley of the shadow of death, I will fear no evil: for Thou art with me; thy rod and thy staff they comfort me. You prepare a table before me in the presence of my enemies; You anoint my head with oil; My cup runs over. Surely goodness and mercy shall follow me all the days of my life; And I will dwell in the house of the Lord forever."

"As if all happiness was not connected with the Practice of Virtue, which necessarily depends upon the Knowledge of Truth," Edmund Burke explains in 1756. "That is, upon the Knowledge of those unalterable Relations which Providence has ordained that everything should bear to every other. These Relations, which are Truth itself, the Foundation of Virtue, and consequently, the only Measures of Happiness." (1)

I believe that without God, a person has no real roots. I don't mean genealogy; I refer to being grounded. A Christian knows there is a higher power and that God has a purpose for our lives. If we follow Him and believe in His Word, we know that in the end, everything will be ok. That faith serves to ground a person because we are in this world but not of it. God rules.

In the times ahead, I'm afraid we are going to need His rod and His staff to comfort us. In the following chapters when we address what we should be doing, it is important to remember that we will be swimming against the tide. Without His strength, His guiding hand and comfort we may weather any storm that comes our way. Through our faith He will restore our souls and lead us in the paths of righteousness. It is also impossible to lead others both in faith and to faith, both of which we may be called upon soon to do, if we are not ourselves straight and strong in our own faith. If we are living in glass houses, we shouldn't be throwing stones.

I call it "carrying your lunch pail." I turn to the story of David and Goliath in the Old Testament.

> **1 Samuel 17:17–20** Now Jesse said to his son David, "Take this ephah of roasted grain and these ten loaves of bread for your brothers and hurry to their camp. Take along these ten cheeses to the commander of their unit. See how your brothers are and bring back some

> assurance from them. They are with Saul and all the men of Israel in the Valley of Elah, fighting against the Philistines."
>
> Early in the morning David left the flock in the care of a shepherd, loaded up and set out, as Jesse had directed. He reached the camp as the army was going out to its battle positions, shouting the war cry.

In the story, David's dad gave him food to take to his brothers serving in the army. The next we hear, David reaches the camp. We don't hear about the journey. David didn't know he was on his way to fight Goliath and fulfill his destiny. David had faith in his father and followed instructions. We don't hear about the stubbed toes and getting lost and David being thirsty as he walked under the hot sun. We don't hear about all the things that may have gone wrong on the journey. That's how it is with us, too. We may stumble, trip, and get lost along the way, but if we listen to God's Word and follow it, in the end we'll fulfill God's purpose for our lives. That is faith. God loves us.

God is love. I believe all earthly love comes from God. It is from and through God, and He gives man his capacity to truly love one another. One cannot truly love another without God. So if you deny God's existence—or worse, acknowledge God's or Christ's existence and then deny His divinity—how can you receive, obtain, or share the love that *is* God?

I was saved late in life. I loved God, believed in Him, and had faith since a very young age. I went to church, attended Catholic school, and believed the Gospel. But I didn't come to know God or Jesus Christ until after my second marriage failed. Then I truly accepted Him into my heart. And *wham*—I really fell in love, truly in love, for the first time in my life.

That's because finally God's grace came to little ol' me, or at least I finally became aware and conscious of the grace He always had waiting for me. It was through God and my Savior Jesus Christ that I finally received the gift of not only my love for Him and His love for me but also the gift of love to give to someone else. Wow, what a life-changing difference it really makes. Nothing compares to really being in love with someone.

> **Romans 8:37–39** No, in all these things we are more than conquerors through Him who loved us. For I am sure that neither death nor life, nor angels nor rulers, nor things present nor things to come, nor powers, nor height nor depth, nor anything else in all creation, will be able to separate us from the love of God in Christ Jesus our Lord.

Love that comes from God and then through us to be given away, whether it is love for your children or romantic and spiritual love, will survive everything this world can throw at it. The house might burn down. You might wreck the car or lose your job. But true love will survive.

> **1 Corinthians 13:4–8** Love is patient and kind; love does not envy or boast; it is not arrogant or rude. It does not insist on its own way; it is not irritable or resentful; it does not rejoice at wrongdoing, but rejoices with the truth. Love bears all things, believes all things, hopes all things, endures all things. Love never ends.

You might feel something you may call love, but without God's grace, I don't believe you can truly be *in* love. However dear love is, its value isn't realized until it is given away. And you can't truly give something away that you do not have. I don't see how someone can deny God and His son Jesus Christ in one breath and then profess their love for someone else in the next.

We have to remember too that Love is a verb. Love is also "do."

> **James 2:14–26** What *does it* profit, my brethren, if someone says he has faith but does not have works? Can faith save him? If a brother or sister is naked and destitute of daily food, and one of you says to them, "Depart in peace, be warmed and filled," but you do not give them the things which are needed for the body, what *does it* profit? Thus also faith by itself, if it does not have works, is dead.

In this scripture, it would also be true if we interchange the word love for faith. What does it profit if someone says he has love but does not have works?

Love without deeds is dead. What I mean is this: if one truly has God's love flowing through him to another to whom he says, "I love you," the works, or the acts, come naturally.

And if you think about it, the words faith and love are often pretty much interchangeable. You are faithful to your wife or husband because of your love for them.

> **Deuteronomy 7:9** Know therefore that the LORD your God is God, the faithful God who keeps covenant and steadfast love with those who love him and keep his commandments, to a thousand generations.

We have faith in God because we know He loves us and wants us to be prosperous and happy and to live fulfilling lives in Him.

As I found out when I really fell in love for the first time, the person I fell in love with suddenly became naturally and effortlessly first in my thoughts, my priorities, and my actions—first after the source of my love to begin with, Christ. It would be simply impossible for me to have the capacity to really, really love someone if I didn't first receive that love from God.

If you were in love, truly in love, you would never have to tell the person that you love them. They would know. It's like that song by the band Extreme:

> Sayin' I love you
> Is not the words I want to hear from you
> It's not that I want you
> Not to say it, but if you only knew
> How easy it would be to show me how you feel
> More than words is all you have to do to make it real
> Then you wouldn't have to say that you love me
> Cause I'd already know
> What would you do if my heart was torn in two?
> More than words to show you feel
> That your love for me is real

What would you say if I took those words away?
Then you couldn't make things new
Just by saying I love you

If all you did was say the words "I love you" without the deeds, without the works, the object of your love would likely always doubt your honesty. There would be a disconnect between what you say and what you do. There would be something profound missing from the relationship. If your spouse were to lose every dime in the bank playing craps at the casino or have an affair and then come home and say, "I love you," would you believe it? I don't believe the works naturally happen unless you are truly in love. I don't believe you can truly, truly be *in* love without God. But when that happens, when you are truly in love, faithfulness is natural.

Do we make mistakes? Of course; we are imperfect human beings. We stumble, trip and fall sometimes.

But when both members of a couple love God and Jesus Christ and have God's love flowing through them and then give it to each other, they have the bond Christ described:

> **Matthew 19:6** For this reason a man shall leave his father and mother and be joined to his wife, and the two shall become one flesh? So they are no longer two, but one flesh. What therefore God has joined together, let no man put asunder.

The joining together isn't a ceremony. It is neither a decree nor proclamation by a court of man. The joining together is God's love first given to each, the man and woman separately, and then to both joined together as one. That love is inseparable. That love survives all things. That love comes from God. That love is eternal. That love is also rare.

But wait, you're saying, "I thought this was a book about politics. What's all this?" It's like the grandson in the movie *The Princess Bride*. "They're kissing again. Do we have to read the kissing parts?" Ok, ok, you're right; this *is* a book about politics, even the kissing parts. Love is the foundation of a solid marriage. Solid marriages build solid families, and solid families are the foundation of strong and solid communities. Again turning to the teachings of Cicero,

> The first bond of union is that between husband and wife; the next, that between parents and children; then we find one home, with everything in common. And this is the foundation of civil government, the nursery, as it were, of the state. (2)

As with a house, if the foundation is rotten, the whole structure is likely to collapse. And let's face it, our families are under threat; many of them are downright rotten.

This is a job for two parents. Each parent, both the mother and the father, have a special role in the household, in the marriage, and as parents. Both are equally vital. This is not to say that a single-parent household will automatically be in disarray or a failure. Many single-parent households can raise successful children, but that's not how it was meant to be. Both are important. Marriage is important. Our founders knew this too. Marriage is the bedrock of society.

A friend of Benjamin Franklin was contemplating not getting married in favor of taking a mistress. Ben wrote him to say, "Don't do it; get married" and here's why:

> Marriage is the proper remedy. It is the most natural state of man, and therefore the state in which you are most likely to find solid happiness. Your reasons against entering into it at present appear to me not well founded. The circumstantial advantages you have in view by postponing it are not only uncertain, but they are small in comparison with that of the thing itself, the being married and settled. It is the man and woman united that make the complete human being. Separate, she wants his force of body and strength of reason; he, her softness, sensibility, and acute discernment. Together they are more likely to succeed in the world. A single man has not nearly the value

> he would have in that state of union. He is an incomplete animal. He resembles the odd half of a pair of scissors. If you get a prudent, healthy wife, your industry in your profession, with her good economy, will be a fortune sufficient." (3)

"A woman cannot bring up a family," says Roy Masters, radio talk show host, author, and director and founder of the Foundation of Human Understanding of the Brighton Academy. "Only a very rare woman can. And she has to be very, very God-centered." I don't agree with everything Roy says, but I'm with him on this one. This isn't a negative statement about women. It is a positive statement about families and about how the role of each parent is different and necessary for raising a family. Let me give you a simple example.

I remember that it was still dark that morning. I was alternately standing, pacing, and sitting in the living room, waiting for my dad to get up and get ready. He was taking me out in the canoe! I must have been seven or eight years old, and this was a huge deal. It was the first time my dad was taking me out in the canoe, just me and him. I was the youngest of four kids in the house, and one-on-one time with my dad was at a premium.

After packing up our gear, a boxed lunch, rods, and reels, having tied the canoe onto the top of his old jeep, off we went. The drive took absolutely forever from our hometown of Ogdensburg, New York, up to the Adirondack Mountains and his hunting camp at Barney Pond. We stopped for a bite at a small gas station in South Colton, where they had homemade doughnuts every day, before finishing up the last few miles to the camp.

It was a near perfect day! I didn't catch any fish. I tipped the canoe, and all our gear—well, my dad's gear—went straight to the bottom. And we forgot the ice and drank sunbaked soda with our warm sandwiches. But none of that mattered. I'll never forget that day out on the pond, just me and my dad. I think I treasure that experience now more than I did at the time.

Time with my mom was special too. But it was special in a different way. The whole vibe was palpably different when I was with my mom than it was with my dad. The conversations were different. The entire mood was different when I was with my dad than with my mom. It was a little more gruff and rough around the edges, more manly. Not better, necessarily, but decidedly different. That's because moms and dads have a decidedly different role within the family.

Why are we talking about family and the roles of the parents? Simple. Again, strong, moral, virtuous, and spiritual families form the foundation for strong communities. Strong, moral, and virtuous communities form the foundation for strong towns, states, and nations. If the foundation of our nation is rotten, how would we expect anything else to be strong?

Strong families start with strong marriages founded on the love between the husband and wife. It all flows downward from there. Have you ever seen a family in which the husband and wife just don't click? They argue often, even in front of the kids, and just don't seem to be right for each other? The marriage is fundamentally unhappy. In that kind of unfortunate situation, are the kids happy? Generally not. It all starts with the love shared between the husband and wife. And that love starts with their love of and faith in God. That makes for a strong marriage and strong family.

What is marriage? The definition of this word, marriage, has meant one man and one woman for many millennium. Recently, the definition of this word has been up for debate, and courts have ruled it no longer means what it has always meant.

According to the New Testament, the disciples asked Jesus this same question. His answer came from scripture.

> **Matthew 19:4–6** Have you not read that He who made them at the beginning made them male and female and said "For this reason a man shall leave his father and mother and be joined to his wife, and the two shall become one flesh." So then, they are no longer two but one flesh. Therefore what God has joined together, let not man separate.

This scripture and its message aren't "anti" anyone or anything. The message is pro-family, pro-children, pro–civil society. The concept and practice of traditional marriage form the bedrock on which a free society is built. The traditional nuclear family produces children. A household with a mother and a father is as God intended. And within the household, the husband and father has a different role than the wife and mother.

Let's start with the husband. The Bible makes it clear that the husband's first job is to be the leader in his household. Don't mistake this to mean he is to be the dictator to rule over his family. It is his responsibility to guide, provide for, and protect his wife and children. It is more a role of influence than rule. He leads by example. The family should respect and trust the father because they know that he loves them, would give or do anything for them, and has only their very best interest at heart.

If a husband and father is doing his job right, he will earn the trust and faith of his family. But he has to earn it. This also comes from God. Ideally, before a man becomes a husband or a father, his first love will be for our Father in heaven. If so, then he will assume his rightful place and role in the family.

Think back to your own childhood. Remember those long road trips? Maybe you were out late and driving home after dark. You were in the backseat. Ever fall asleep? You weren't afraid. You just somehow knew you'd get home ok. You just knew that your parents knew the way home and would get you there safe and sound. You had faith in them. You just knew they loved you and would take care of you. That is how it is when a husband and dad is doing his job as the leader of his family. It is a relationship based not on fear but on respect, trust and mutual love.

> **1 Peter 3:7** You husbands in the same way, live with your wives in an understanding way, as with someone weaker, since she is a woman; and show her honor as a fellow heir of the grace of life, so that your prayers will not be hindered.
> **1 Corinthians 13:4–6** Love is patient, love is kind. It does not envy, it does not boast, it is not proud. It does not dishonor others, it is not self-seeking, it is not easily angered, it keeps no record of wrongs. Love does not delight in evil but rejoices with the truth.

The husband loves his wife. He honors and respects her. His earthly world revolves around her, and he protects, cares for, and provides for her. He becomes one flesh with her. If his love for his wife flows from God's grace and he truly becomes one flesh with his love, then he won't abuse her, cheat, lie, or command obedience. They become partners. But it is his job to lead.

When I was a young, single soldier, I lived in the barracks with the guys and could party as hard as any of my buddies. We'd hit the town and have a few too many drinks, occasionally get into relatively harmless fights, and chase girls. We never hurt anyone or got arrested, and we always made it back to the unit in time for formation.

All of that changed when I got married, and especially when I became a dad. I thought, "What if something were to happen in the middle of the night, and right when my family needed me, I was drunk?" That would have been totally unacceptable. I would have never forgiven myself. It was a matter of personal honor, and I would have been ashamed of myself. So it never happened. I was never drunk again. I'm a dad. Things are different from when I was all I had to worry about.

And as far as being a father, nothing teaches your kids better than your example. You will raise what you are. If you take drugs, your kids will too. If you drink, your kids will too. If you beat your wife, it is very likely that your sons will grow up to beat their wives, and despite their efforts to do otherwise, your daughters will likely marry husbands who do not respect them and will slap them around too.

The basic rule of thumb is to be the man you want your sons to become and the man you want your daughters to marry. That all starts with your love for your wife. And the way you love your wife starts with God.

> **Ephesians 5:25** Husbands, love your wives, as Christ loved the church and gave himself up for her.

But as a man, you have to earn your place in the family, all the time. We had a saying in the Army. One "oh, crap" can erase 1000 "Thatta boys." To me, the definition of man is one who is responsible, loving, compassionate, protective, and morally strong, defending his convictions. It's a tall order. I don't do it all the time every day either. But it all comes with the job. A good man will accept it all—not as a challenge or rite of passage but just as part of the territory.

Dads and men in general are getting a bad rap these days. Turn on just about any sitcom, and you'll see what I mean. Almost universally, the dad is portrayed as the bumbling but good-natured dork. He really doesn't know what's going on in the house and is always screwing things up. That's unfortunate because that is not what men are supposed to be. I hope that with so many kids growing up in single-parent households today and without a father in their lives, we aren't going to create wholesale generations of young boys who never learn how to be men.

I fear that many boys see only the worst examples of what men are supposed to be. If the men in the lives even tried to live up to their obligations as men in our households and in our families, how many of those destructive rioters burning down and looting businesses on the streets of Ferguson or Baltimore would have participated in that orgy of violence? Most likely not nearly as many.

What about the godly wife? What is her role? Some men will say the wife is to be subservient to the husband, that she is subordinate to the man in a marriage. I am of the opinion that isn't the case at all. No, I believe that man and wife are an inseparable team. Will they always agree on everything all the time? Doubtful. The team of husband and wife serve the Lord first and then each other. As such, she is his closest confidant, advisor, best friend, and supporter, just as the husband is to her.

There is a popular social media post that shows what I mean. It goes something like this:

> An English professor wrote a sentence on the blackboard: "A woman without her man is nothing." He then asked his students to punctuate it. The male students wrote, "A woman, without her man, is nothing." The female students had a different answer: "A woman: without her, man is nothing." The lesson here is twofold. Both are correct, and that's the point.

> **Proverbs 31:10–31** An excellent wife who can find? She is far more precious than jewels. The heart of her husband trusts in her, and he will have no lack of gain. She does him good, and not harm, all the days of her life. She seeks wool and flax, and works with willing hands. She is like the ships of the merchant; she brings her food from afar.

At the risk of being redundant, it all starts with a true love shared between them. If a man is a godly man and loves the Lord and through God's grace loves his wife, his wife will never have anything to fear in him. Likewise, if the love is returned in the same manner from his wife, the team has a strong union. He has earned her trust and her faithfulness. Thus, he has earned the position of leader because she knows everything she gives to her husband is returned—respect, trust, loyalty, and love. Teamwork. Doesn't mean it's easy, but it is solid.

> **Ephesians 5:22–6:9** Wives, submit to your own husbands, as to the Lord. For the husband is the head of the wife even as Christ is the head of the church, his body, and is himself its Savior. Now as the church submits to Christ, so also wives should submit in everything to their husbands. Husbands, love your wives, as Christ loved the church and gave himself up for her, that he might sanctify her, having cleansed her by the washing of water with the word.

The man, before he becomes the husband, has to be worthy of her trust, respect, faithfulness, and love. Submit doesn't mean submissive, in my humble opinion. It is a matter of trust, respect, and faith. She believes in her husband and from his love for her, he would give his everything to do right by her and never let her down.

> **Ephesians 5:33** However, let each one of you love his wife as himself, and let the wife see that she respects her husband.

As Christ loved each of us and gave His life for our salvation, the man has to "love his wife as himself" so that she knows his heart and that she is first in his life, after the Lord Himself.

Ok, I'm done with the family stuff. We're done with the "kissing parts." I can sum it all up in this: God is first. Next comes your spouse. Then come your children, followed by everyone and everything else. That is a strong family on which to build a strong society and a strong nation. However, it all starts with a strong you. Ok, now I'm done.

One last thing: seek the fellowship of others in faith. Like keeping the Sabbath holy (we discuss the Ten Commandments next), finding the fellowship of others also restores the soul and will strengthen us for any trial.

> **Hebrews 10:24-25** and let us consider how to stimulate one another to love and good deeds, not forsaking our own assembling together, as is the habit of some, but encouraging one another; and all the more as you see the day drawing near.

# 6

# The Ten Commandments

**"The strength of our country is the strength of its religious convictions. The foundations of our society and our government rest so much on the teachings of the Bible that it would be difficult to support them if faith in these teachings would cease to be practically universal in our country."**

**— Calvin Coolidge**

When people speak of God's wrath, often the immediate image is of Sodom and Gomorrah, with fire bolts falling indiscriminately from the sky, destroying whole cities and anyone and everyone. Real fire and brimstone stuff. Is that what God wants of us? Did God create us to be His minions and slaves? Is He like Sister Mary Stigmata, a.k.a. The Penguin, with her ruler in the movie *The Blues Brothers*, ready to smack us around at the first misstep?

In the Old Testament, God first gave His rules to Moses on Mount Sinai. According to the Book of Exodus, God revealed the Ten Commandments as the law for His chosen people to follow. At face value, these Commandments seem very limiting and demanding. However, in fact God's commandments are very liberating. Following God's law allows the believer to be free. Free from torment, jealousy, retribution, and revenge from others and free to accept God's love. Then we are free to share God's love with others. God is love, and our capacity to love one another comes from God. That is very liberating.

God had just freed the Israelites from enslavement under the pharaoh in Egypt. Through Moses, He parted the Red Sea to allow the Israelites to escape. Why then, just as His people were free, would He have them go through all of that just to enslave them Himself under tyrannical rules?

Imagine, if you will, that each of these rules was followed by the words "so that." You would see that God does not want us to be blind servants and subjects; He wants us to be free and happy in this life. Then He wants us to join Him in the paradise of Heaven in the next life as well.

But wait, you might be asking, "Just what do the Ten Commandments have to do with freedom in America?" The short answer is, "Everything!"

God's commandments lay out the ground-rules for not only personal conduct in relations between you and God, but also for conduct between each other. If everyone faithfully followed God's law, there would be no need for any government, police, or armies. As it is, man is imperfect and subject to all the temptations this earth throws at us. As a result, much of our modern criminal and even civil law has their roots deep in the Ten Commandments. The Ten Commandments were also the basis of our modern law. That's why until recently many of our courthouses displayed plaques of the Ten Commandments. These displays served as a reminder of where our very concept of law originated.

God gave us these rules thousands of years ago through his servant, Moses. These commandments are still a very good set of guidelines by which to conduct our lives. Honor, love and praise God. Take some time for yourself to rest. Don't steal your neighbor's stuff, kill him or try to sleep with his wife.

Don't waste your time being jealous of someone else and the things they may have. Pretty simple.

As James Madison so eloquently stated in Federalist 51, "*If* men were *angels, no government* would be necessary." Unfortunately men are not angels. So it seems that in any discussion of forming a society among imperfect men, according to God's law, the Ten Commandments is a logical starting point.

Jesus Christ gave us only two commandments.

> **Mark 12:29–31** The first of all the commandments is this: "Hear, O Israel, the Lord our God, the Lord is One. And you shall love the Lord your God with all your heart, with all your soul, and with all your mind, and with all your strength." This is the first commandment. And the second, like it, is this: "You shall love your neighbor as yourself." There is no other commandment greater than these.

If we imperfect, mortal humans could only do that during our short time spent on this earth, all would be fine. We'd respect each other's stuff, privacy, family, and "life, liberty, and pursuit of happiness." We'd be, as Madison described, angels.

One incredible thing about the Ten Commandments is that no matter what race, creed, or religion you are from, they apply perfectly to every human being on Earth. They are not just laws for you to obey. They also list what you don't want anyone else to do to you. Even if you don't believe in God, you don't want your spouse taken from you. You don't want to be stolen from; you don't want to be lied to or killed.

When we have no other gods before Him, loving Him with all our heart, we do not make or worship any idols, and we show real love for each other, genuinely treating others the way we want to be treated. Thus, we do not break the other Commandments. I won't sleep with your wife because I don't want you to sleep with mine. I won't kill you because I don't want you to kill me. I won't lie to you because I don't want you to lie to me, and so on.

As we go through the Ten Commandments, we'll add the "so that," and we'll see just how liberating God's law truly can be.

1. You shall have no other gods before Me, *so that* you can find God's grace and find happiness in your life and faith to inherit God's kingdom in the next life.

The first commandment is about loyalty. "Other gods" doesn't refer only to the golden calf or carved image; they can be anything that distracts you from following God and pursuing His purpose in your life. Addictions to drugs, alcohol, or even pornography can keep you from God's grace. These earthly and destructive things will cloud your judgment and occupy your thoughts and your time. I'm going to assume that we are not worshiping other gods such as the moon, stars or "Mother Earth." Those, of course are explicitly prohibited for obvious reasons. We should not allow anything to come between us and God's grace.

Nothing can compare to finding God's grace. When our lives become cluttered with other things, it is easy to become distracted from honoring our Creator. Don't fall into that trap. For the patriot, remember that He endowed us with our rights.

2. You shall not make for yourself a carved image, or any likeness of anything that is in heaven above, or that is in the earth beneath, or that is in the water under the earth; you shall not bow down to them nor serve them *so that* your heart will remain pure and available for God's grace.

The second commandment is about worship. We cannot worship two gods. Remember the Israelites worshiping the golden calf when Moses came off the mountain? We can't worship both the calf and God. Even in church when we see the sculptures of Mary or paintings, Stations of the Cross in catholic churches, etc., we are not worshiping the image or the sculpture, we are worshiping God and Jesus Christ.

3. You shall not take the name of the Lord your God in vain *so that* your heart will be open to receive God's grace.

The third commandment is about reverence. You can't possibly use God's holy name as a cuss word and at the same time expect to honor and love God and Christ Jesus. And you can't be a good servant of the Lord and at the same time think so little of Him as to use His name as a swear word. What would you think if your neighbor uttered your name disparagingly every time things didn't go his way and he was frustrated, angry, or upset?

If your neighbor ran over the garden hose with the lawn mower, dropped the groceries in his driveway, wrecked the car, or got into an argument with his wife, and in each instance shouted your name in disdain, would you consider that he thought highly of you? I doubt it. It is the same with God and His son Jesus Christ. This is especially true when you stop and think of just how much He has given you—namely His only son to die on the cross, giving you the chance for everlasting life.

Words are important. You will generally reflect your beliefs in your words. So if you are using God's name as a curse word, are you not cursing Him? If you are cursing Him, how can you honor Him as the Lord our God? How can you love and honor His son, Jesus Christ, as your Lord and Savior if you are using His name as a cursing swear word? It would seem that you can't.

The reverse is also true. Make a conscious effort to no longer use those words and phrases, and your thoughts will follow. Begin to honor and love the Lord through your choice of words, and He will be raised in your conscious mind closer to His rightful place in your life. It's all a matter of respect. He created you. He gave you the chance to obtain everlasting life through the sacrifice of His son, Jesus Christ. You should at least respect Him for that enough not to spit His name out as a curse word.

Then, as your thoughts and words change, perhaps your attitude and behavior will follow. If we begin to honor Him in our words, maybe we will begin to honor Him in our deeds. Words are important. Thoughts and actions will follow.

There are several verses in the Bible that explain cursing and swearing.

**Proverbs 10:32** The lips of the righteous know what is acceptable, but the mouth of the wicked, what is perverse.

> **Colossians 3:8** But now you must put them all away: anger, wrath, malice, slander, and obscene talk from your mouth.
> **Ephesians 4:29** Let no corrupting talk come out of your mouths, but only such as is good for building up, as fits the occasion, that it may give grace to those who hear.

Though the Bible does not take cursing and swearing lightly, it does not fall under the same parameters as breaking this third commandment. But use your words to encourage, mentor, and lift people up, not to disparage or curse them. Look, I know no one is perfect, including me, but what I am talking about here is the ideal.

4. Remember the Sabbath day, to keep it holy *so that* you can rest, rejuvenate, refocus, and reconnect with God.

The fourth commandment is about sanctification and relationship. The world is hard. It can be cold and heartless, and it is easy to think that nothing is going your way. The car will always break, and so will the refrigerator—and right at the end of the month, too, when there is no money left in the bank to fix it. Disagreements happen with spouses and children. Your boss is too demanding, and you will get stuck in traffic.

That's what happens in this world. We can't fight it every day. If we don't take a day off to reconnect with family, rest, and prepare for the next week to come, we can easily lose focus on what's truly important. Faith, family, freedom, and fun. We need to save at least one day a week for all of those.

While I was stationed as a staff officer in the 10th Mountain Division, my then battalion commander called the time we take to rest and reconnect "sharpening your axe." You can be a hard-charging, ambitious, hardworking stud or studette all week long, metaphorically chopping wood all day every day, but eventually your axe will lose its edge. So will you. You have to stop and sharpen your axe on at least one day per week to stay sharp. It is the same spiritually, too. God wants you to succeed. God wants you to be happy and prosperous and have a full life. You can't properly serve Him if you're worn and tattered. You can't get there with a dull axe or a dull spirit. Take one day a week to sharpen your spiritual axe.

Pray. Go to church. Play with the kids. Have at least one meal together as a family, and talk and listen to each other. Be together. Reconnect with your wife or husband and spend time in the Word. You'll be better for it, and you'll be more prepared to take on all the challenges this world will throw at you. It's an investment that will pay off handsomely.

The tradition of keeping Sunday as a holy day can still be seen throughout our society. Stores open later and close earlier. In many communities the purchase of alcohol is restricted on Sundays and bars are closed. In our national heritage, Sundays are days of worship, family and rest. Good. I hope it stays that way. I sincerely hope that the hustle and bustle of our daily lives can be held at bay to allow us one day to sharpen our axe.

5. Honor your father and your mother *so that* love and obedience to the Almighty God will reign in your house.

The fifth commandment is about respect for parental authority. God has established a beautiful system for the family and loving household. Not to be redundant, but this is based on the assumption that the father and mother are in love both with the Lord and with each other. The father of the house will love the Lord and keep His Word. As such, he becomes the representative of God in the house to guide, mentor, and lead the family to Christ. To his children, the father has the obligation, again, to be the man he wants his sons to become and the man he wants his daughters to marry. He carries that obligation with him every day. No days off when he is setting the example for his family.

So even though this commandment says to "honor your father and your mother," there is an obligation, first, for the father to be an honorable man of God.

Radio Talk Show Host Mike Church has a very good explanation of this commandment and the implications it has in the family. "The father and the mother have to cooperate with one another and then with Almighty God to make the child," Mike says. "This is beautiful. The child then has to cooperate with this act and then must honor the father and the mother. This is so perfect of a system," he continues, "it cannot have happened by accident." (1)

The commandment to honor your father and your mother is one of obedience. It is an obligation—boy, there is that word again, *obligation.* But there is an obligation for the parents to lead the children in Christ's teachings, and their actions come from love. But there is also an obligation for the parents to discipline the children when they go astray. Honoring your parents also means obeying them as they make corrections in your behavior. Everyone makes mistakes, especially when we are learning something new. Kids are always learning. Parents who have the love of the Holy Spirit flowing through them will discipline and make corrections, instilling lessons in the children. The children obey. They honor their parents and learn.

With good teachers—parents—the kids will learn not only how to behave as kids but also how to parent when it is their turn. The bottom line is that parents have only one job—to make it so their kids don't need them. When you have accepted the responsibility of having children, you have accepted the responsibility of raising them to be productive, caring adults and parents in the Lord in their own right.

This also means that the kids continue to honor their parents in their old age. Raising kids is hard and expensive. Good parents sacrifice a *lot* for their kids. When the kids are adults and the parents need someone to watch over them and maybe even provide and care for them, the children need to honor their parents' sacrifices and be there.

Think of the system that is in place when this commandment is followed! First, you have a mother and a father who are in love with the Lord and with each other. They raise their kids by setting the example of nurturing, caring for, and guiding their children as they grow to be responsible adults in Christ so they will raise their family in the same way. Then, as the parents age, they are taken care of by their family, who honors and loves them in accordance with God's teachings. It's a very perfect system for not only perpetuating a loving, spiritual, God-fearing family but also for creating and perpetuating the same in society. If only every family obeyed and followed this commandment. Think of what this world would look like and how we would act toward each other. If only.

As Mike says, "It cannot have happened by accident." (2)

6. You shall not murder *so that* you are not murdered yourself and you may live your life to the fullest in accordance with God's plan.

The sixth commandment is about respect for human life. This one shouldn't need any further discussion. Murder is bad. The taking of another life is about the worst act one can commit. Like Clint Eastwood's character, Will Munny, says in the hit movie *The Unforgiven*, "It's a hell of a thing, killing a man. Take away all he's got and all he's ever gonna have."

If you murder someone, what happens next? Think of the pain, sorrow, grief, and suffering you will inflict on the victim's family. Where does the authority come from that allows you to cause so much pain for people? Certainly it does not come from God.

We should clarify that murder is different from some other kinds of killing. I know it sounds hypocritical in terms of this commandment, but in war, soldiers are required to kill. That's a different topic. I know as a former soldier that we went out of our way to minimize unjustified death, commonly called collateral damage. But destroying the enemy is necessary in war. Whether in the big picture the war itself is justified may be debatable, but the individual soldier thrown into the fray is held blameless.

For example, Hamas and Palestinian fighters in Gaza will fire hundreds of rockets at Israeli civilian targets to include shopping centers, housing areas, and schools. When the Israelis go looking for the rocket launchers to destroy them, they find that the Palestinians intentionally position themselves among civilians. The Palestinians shoot rockets and mortars from the rooftops of apartment buildings from school yards and parks. If the Israelis bomb these rockets to protect their people, who is committing murder? Is it the Israelis who defensively are protecting their civilians and are forced to take out the rockets and in the process may kill civilians? Or is it the Palestinians who purposefully fire rockets from places where their own people are likely to end up in the line of fire?

As Israeli Prime Minister Benjamin Netanyahu says, "We use our missiles to protect our people; they use people to protect their missiles."

But let's get back to the commandments. Again, if you murder someone, what happens next? Well, of course it is a crime. You most likely will get caught. Then off you go to prison. Maybe for life. Now you've denied two families a loved one. The family of the one you killed and now your own because you rot in prison for the rest of your life. Great move. Or, maybe you'll get the death penalty.

Maybe, just maybe, you'll get away with it scot free. But are you really free? You'll spend the rest of your life always wondering if you'll get caught. You'll spend the rest of your life looking over your shoulder, nervous about getting found out, living with a horrendous secret. Is that freedom? Following the commandment *thou shalt not murder* is freedom from all of the above.

Your soul is also free of the guilt, regret, and shame that committing the sin should dump on you.

> **Matthew 6:14–15** For if you forgive men when they sin against you, your heavenly Father will also forgive you. But if you do not forgive men their sins, your Father will not forgive your sins.

Pursuing revenge will eat you up from the inside, as will filling up with anger, resentment, and hatred. Forgiveness is hard, but it is also very liberating. Forgiving someone who has wronged you doesn't mean you are suddenly new best friends. You probably won't be sharing box seats at the Yankees game. But forgiveness, true forgiveness, frees you of all the negative emotions you're carrying around.

Of course, not murdering also means not being the target of revenge yourself.

> **Leviticus 24:17–18** Whoever takes a human life shall surely be put to death.

7. You shall not commit adultery *so that* you will love, respect, and honor your spouse in the way God teaches.

The seventh commandment is about purity in relationships. Committing adultery is usually a lot of work. There's the sneaking around, lying, covering up, and guilt. It takes a lot of time and money. Then you have cover up and hide any money that disappears. Adultery is an affront to God on many levels. It is lying to your spouse and your family.

The basic building block of all societies is the family. To commit adultery destroys families. It leads to wrecked marriages and divorce. Nothing good can come to a family, a community, or a society when the basic trust, honor, and love between a married couple is violated and destroyed. Faithfulness within marriages secures households, which helps to secure society. Adulterous relationships rot out the foundation of our country.

I think it would be better to invest that time, attention and energy into our current relationship than to hop to the presumably greener grass over the fence.

In the military under their Uniform Code of Military Justice, adultery is still a crime. In the past, adultery was seen as so egregious as to warrant being stoned to death in the public square. We don't do that anymore. That's a good thing but adultery is still very destructive to the family and to the community.

8. You shall not steal *so that* private property rights are respected, a free market can exist in our society, and you are free from punishment and revenge.

The eighth commandment is about honesty. Free market capitalism depends on private property rights and liberty. Private property rights depend on this commandment. You are free to pursue other interests, including having a home in which you can store your belongings and being able to leave your home to go to work or the movies because of the basic respect of private property. I can't just steal your stuff. If anarchy existed and there were no respect for private property, you'd have to stand guard over your food and other belongings. To not do so would invite raiders and thieves to steal everything you own.

We teach this commandment to our kids. "Did your sister have the blue crayon first? Well, give it back to her."

Unfortunately, stealing still happens all too often, and that is one of the cases in which we task government to step in to both prevent the crime and punish offenders. By not stealing as a matter of course in our relations with others, we can have the expectation that our property will be respected as well.

Stealing, theft, burglary, breaking and entering, and the like are all in our criminal code. There was a time in ancient history when stealing would get your hand cut off. Stealing horses in the old west could mean a hanging from the nearest tree limb. This commandment also covers such things as extortion, patent infringement, stealing copyrights and trademarks.

I have to mention again here that citizens cannot delegate to government powers that they themselves do not possess. Often we'll here someone say government has the right or no right to do this or that. Government doesn't have rights. It only has power. We can't empower government to steal on our behalf. Frédéric Bastiat, the nineteenth-century economist, called this legal plunder.

> But how is this legal plunder to be identified? Quite simply. See if the law takes from some persons what belongs to them and gives it to other persons to whom it does not belong. See if the law benefits one citizen at the expense of another by doing what the citizen himself cannot do without committing a crime.
>
> —Frédéric Bastiat, *The Law* (3)

If our committing an act would constitute a crime, then allowing our legislators to pass a law granting the state the power to do it on our behalf, enforcing it against our neighbors, also constitutes a crime. Such a crime would be in violation of both the Constitution and the Ten Commandments and is therefore null and void. Or at least it should be. But we both know we have empowered government to commit crimes on our behalf hundreds, if not thousands, of times.

9. You shall not bear false witness against your neighbor *so that* you will be a person of integrity and honor in all your personal and professional dealings.

The ninth commandment is about truthfulness. Any society based on liberty and our God-given rights relies on honesty. We have to have a level of certainty that the folks we are dealing with are being truthful and honest. Contracts and our other business dealings require it. Truth has to permeate every facet of our lives.

Slander and libel are crimes in our penal code too. Fraud, breach of contracts and a host of other civil and criminal laws have at the foundation the 9th Commandment.

10. You shall not covet your neighbor's goods, his wife, or anything that is your neighbor's *so that* you won't conduct yourself based on comparison of yourself with others.

The tenth commandment is about contentment. It isn't at all healthy to crave or improperly desire what isn't yours. In your personal relationships, if you're spending time coveting your neighbor's wife, you're neglecting your own. Live your life, counting your blessings with what you have instead of focusing on what the other guy has. Do what's right by you and your family, keep faith in God, and get up every morning and do your very best. Remember, God does want you to prosper.

God has given each of us a separate and special set of abilities. We have the capacity to live full, spiritual, and prosperous lives. We really have an obligation to employ those gifts and talents that God has given us to the best of our ability to honor Him. That would be impossible if we are constantly more worried about what our neighbors have than about employing our talents to improve our lives and those of our families.

Covetousness leads to jealousy, resentment, and distrust between neighbors. Those emotions lead only to the negative expense of energy that helps no one.

Imagine for a moment the society that would exist if we all could obey these commandments. I realize this is a fantasy, and I am a realist. But here is the connection between our rights and the Ten Commandments: if none of us ever broke a commandment, we would have no need for government. We really only need a government at all when someone breaks a commandment against us and therefore violates our rights. If someone steals my stuff, I want a representative of government to show up with a badge and get my stuff back.

These commandments and our penal code that essentially is derived from them, are critical to our functioning civil society. As a republic, we are a nation of law, not of men, meaning that our laws, our commandments apply equally to all, regardless of wealth, station, poverty, who you know or what public office you may hold. At least that is how it is supposed to be.

# 7

## The Bill of Rights

**"If you love wealth more than liberty, the tranquility of servitude better than the animating contest of freedom, depart from us in peace. We ask not your counsel nor your arms. Crouch down and lick the hand that feeds you. May your chains rest lightly upon you and may posterity forget that you were our countrymen."**

— Samuel Adams

Of course our founding documents, the Declaration of Independence and the Constitution, spell out much more than just laws. They define our basic worth as citizens, our rights that cannot be infringed upon, and the functions and organization of our government.

The Declaration of Independence spells out what the just and correct relationship between government and the citizen should be. Referencing that remarkable document again, it states the following:

> When in the Course of human events, it becomes necessary for one people to dissolve the political bands which have connected them with another, and to assume among the powers of the earth, the separate and equal station to which the Laws of Nature and of Nature's God entitle them, a decent respect to the opinions of mankind requires that they should declare the causes which impel them to the separation.

Laws of Nature Nature's God, or God's law. To what are we entitled? What did Thomas Jefferson mean? A New England preacher explained the concept in this way: "The law of nature (or those rules of behavior which the Nature God has given men…fit and necessary to the welfare of mankind) is the law and will of the God of nature, which all men are obliged to obey…The law of nature, which is the Constitution of the God of nature, is universally obliging. It varies not with men's humors or interests, but is immutable as the relations of things" (Abraham Williams, Election Sermon, Boston, 1762).

This concept was furthered fourteen years later, again in our Declaration of Independence:

> We hold these truths to be self-evident, that all men are created equal, that they are endowed by their Creator with certain unalienable Rights, that among these are Life, Liberty and the pursuit of Happiness.—That to secure these rights, Governments are instituted among Men, deriving their just powers from the consent of the governed.

From the consent of the governed. That's us. We are the governed. Just how much of what the government has been doing lately have you willfully consented to? Did anyone ask you before the NSA started scanning our e-mails, monitoring our phone calls, and collecting mass metadata on all Americans, even those who hadn't committed any crime? Have you consented to being groped at the airport by inefficient and ineffective government employees every time you try to get on an airplane? Have you consented to billions of your tax dollars being shifted to private corporations in subsidies while the government chooses which businesses should survive and which ones should fail despite how they may perform in the free market? No? I don't either.

> There are two potential violators of man's rights: the criminals and the government. The great achievement of the United States was to draw a distinction between these two—by forbidding to the second the legalized version of the activities of the first.
>
> —Ayn Rand

The Bill of Rights constitutes the first ten amendments to the US Constitution. The new states would not ratify the Constitution until these guarantees were purposefully written in to protect the God-given rights of "we the people." These men had just fought a war against an all-powerful king. They held a fundamental distrust for government, and for good reason.

The tendency throughout history is that once people are in positions of power, they like to stay there. Sons have killed their own fathers to gain power, brother has killed brother, nations have gone to war, and millions have died so one people, or one man could rule over others. As Lord Acton famously stated, "Power tends to corrupt, and *absolute power corrupts absolutely.* Great men are almost always bad men." (1)

Well, if they don't start out as bad men, they almost always become bad men. America's founders and the Framers of the Constitution knew this. They had suffered under ruling kings all their lives. They had enough, declared independence from a king's rule, and were willing to fight for their freedom. This same king sent thousands of men with guns across the ocean to kill the people he ruled. He then fought a war to hold his power over the colonies. The king of England sacrificed about forty-one thousand people on both sides to try to maintain power over the American colonies. In proportion to today's population, American casualties alone during the American War of

Independence would be about three million dead today. All so one man could keep control over another people.

The rights listed in the Declaration of Independence are nonnegotiable. Unalienable. They should be so still. The Bill of Rights was meant to ensure that government, the State, would not become too powerful and that the value of the individual citizen would forever remain paramount in our system.

Unlike the Ten Commandments, while limiting the sinful actions of the individual actually liberate us to live full, prosperous, and happy lives, the Bill of Rights was intended to limit and confine the government lest it become too powerful.

Take this another way. I believe God has a purpose for everyone in this life. If man creates a government that is so overbearing through laws, regulations, taxes, and so on that the citizen becomes preoccupied with obeying government's rules, the citizen cannot devote himself to pursuing God's purpose for his life.

Have you ever really thought about all the things we now have to ask the government's permission to do? So many laws and regulations that carry the weight of law are weighing down on us that it's hard to do almost anything without the consent of government. These laws and regulations come from every level of government — local, state, and federal. Just a short list of things you, as a private citizen, cannot do without the permission of government includes the following:

1. Get married
2. Pull a fish from a pond
3. Fix your porch
4. Install a new toilet in your bathroom
5. Sell lemonade
6. Shoot and eat a deer
7. Start a business
8. Drive your car
9. Sell sandwiches
10. Put your boat in the water

11. Homeschool your kids
12. Trap a skunk under your garage
13. Buy a pistol in most states
14. Dredge a ditch—the EPA will call that an "inland waterway"

The list goes on and on, but you get the point. With all of us living under such a system, can we still really call ourselves free? There was an article recently about the habits of people creating cairns of loose stones in the Adirondack Mountains of New York. The author of the article wanted to ban the practice. So someone thought they were in a position to prohibit others from creating a small pile of stones on top of a mountain. Really? Where did this authority to rule over the harmless actions of others come from?

New York's Department of Conservation actually passed (passed is the wrong word, as no elected official actually voted on it) a regulation that made taking a picture of a fish not in season (for social media) punishable with a fine. It didn't matter in the slightest if that fish was released unharmed or not. You can't make this stuff up. Mind you, the punishment wasn't for killing or eating the fish, but just for taking its picture. Luckily, there was such a public outcry at the lunacy of this the regulation was rescinded.

It was never supposed to be this way. We the people were to be assumed free. That is specifically why the founders insisted on the Bill of Rights and a Constitution limiting the power of government. It cannot be stated often or strongly enough that the Constitution is not a limitation on the private citizen. The Constitution applied only to the federal government to limit its powers. It had nothing whatsoever to do with limiting the freedom or liberty of "we the people." The Bill of Rights specified to government what they must not ever, ever, ever stop the people from doing and what they cannot ever do to us.

Why are we assumed to be free? Because God made us and we answer to Him. As God's creations, we are all equally treasured and valuable. God's law by far supersedes any law of man. It is only when we commit trespasses against our neighbor, or sin, that we get ourselves into trouble. We can't kill a guy, steal his stuff, spread lies—oh, my goodness. Does this list look familiar? It almost mirrors the Ten Commandments!

And that's the point. Just like your neighbor can't legally take your stuff, governments can't do it either. As it says in the Declaration of Independence, the only reason we need government at all is to secure our rights. If everyone could be counted on to do the right thing in every circumstance, we wouldn't need any higher earthly power at all. We, as God's creations, were never meant to be ruled over by other men. Ever. Never. Ever. I can't stress that enough. Governments do *not* rule over us. We, as a free people, created government to do some very limited functions on our behalf. That's it. We are still in charge. It is our government. We made it. At any time of our choosing, we can tear it down and start over. We've done it before. People either conveniently ignore or never knew that we did have a form of government before our constitutional republic. The Articles of Confederation didn't work, so we tore that up and started over.

That's why our Framers put the provisions in our Constitution to amend and change it as we go. Article V of the Constitution tells us how to make changes. And even before the ink was dry on the document, the states insisted on making changes. The fear of an omnipotent government was so prevalent even then that the states would not ratify the Constitution until there were amendments written into it that guaranteed the rights of the people. These rights became our Bill of Rights.

When the Framers had finished their work on September 17, 1787 President Washington attached a letter to the signed draft and sent it to Congress. Congress ratified the Constitution without any changes and sent it to the states. When several of the larger states threatened to reject the Constitution, they were invited to ratify the main body of the Constitution but attach suggested amendments. They submitted 189! At the first session of Congress, these suggested amendments were reduced to 12 by James Madison, and 10 of them were finally approved and ratified by the states. Thus was born America's famous Bill of Rights.

I have to say one more time the fact that these rights are listed in the Constitution does *not* mean they come from government. They were ours to begin with. They were endowed to us by our Creator. We are free and equal because we are creations of God. The amendments are not written for us.

They are written as a reminder and as a legally binding contract between "we the people" and the government we created.

We'll briefly cover the Bill of Rights here. As we do, remember the agenda of the enemy and the actions of his minions here on earth. Are our rights still respected and protected or hallowed as intended? No, they aren't. As the value of our rights is eroded, so is the value of each individual citizen. It is the value, worth, and equality of each individual citizen that set this country apart from the rest of the world. When our value diminishes our country, as it once was, will be gone.

My discussion of the Bill of Rights might seem elementary and based on little more than simple common sense. That's just what I mean to do. I'm not a lawyer. I'm not going ad nauseam into the legalese of the amendments. My intent is to touch on the principles at work that guarantee our rights. Remember, these are limits on *government*, not limits on "we the people."

Also, the preamble to the Constitution starts with this: "We the People of the United States." The Constitution doesn't say, "Everyone residing within the borders of the United States." The Constitution and the rights that it guarantees apply only to American citizens. I know I'll catch a lot of flak over that one, but someone who is not a legal American citizen can't claim all the rights of being one. There is a huge difference between being *in* America and being *an* American.

**First Amendment**: Congress shall make no law respecting an establishment of religion, or prohibiting the free exercise thereof; or abridging the freedom of speech, or of the press; or the right of the people peaceably to assemble, and to petition the Government for a redress of grievances.

Do you see anything in this amendment that says religion will have no place in government? Do you see anything stating that we must stamp all vestiges of God out of our schools, courts, and public squares? Do you see anything saying that churches cannot take a stand on political issues or that the clergy and their congregations can't make public statements on policy? No? I don't either.

All it says is that the federal government cannot establish a religion and that Congress can't pass laws inhibiting or infringing on anyone's right to practice their religion, whatever that may be, however that free citizen chooses. Period. In fact, much of the public discourse leading up to the Revolutionary War took place in our churches. It was our preachers who led the way to freedom.

Now, no matter what the government does up to and including the murder, dismemberment and sale of dead babies funded by the taxpayers, our pulpits by and large are silent. That is a tragedy; again, there is no separation of church and state required in the First Amendment. The federal government cannot make laws regarding religion, but our pastors are certainly not prohibited from speaking out against government.

An explanation of the importance of the freedoms of speech and the press to a representative republic should not be necessary. These were specifically listed to expose all government corruption, lies, crimes, and actions. No actions of government were supposed to be done in secret. There were supposed to be no bills passed that the people didn't know about. The now famous quote from the then house majority leader Nancy Pelosi comes to mind: "We have to pass the bill to find out what is in it."(2)

The media was supposed to be the ultimate watchdogs over government corruption. There was a day when government officials feared true investigative reporters. Remember Watergate? President Nixon resigned the presidency over eight and a half minutes of audio recordings that were erased and proved a government cover-up. That is what the press was for. Think we can count on to be the watchdogs over government now?

The remainder of the First Amendment was put in place so that if government wrongdoings are exposed, we the people can assemble, draft grievances, and send them to our government to be addressed. We are supposed to watch government and our government officials like hawks, and when we find them up to no good we are supposed to pounce on them until it is fixed or they are driven out of office.

**Second Amendment**: A well-regulated militia, being necessary to the security of a free State, the right of the people to keep and bear Arms, shall not be infringed.

Despite what the current political narrative is, the Second Amendment isn't so we can hunt a deer. It isn't even exclusively so we can protect our homes and our families, although that is an important aspect of "shall not be infringed." To have a true understanding of the Second Amendment, it is important to put it into the historical context in which it was written.

America had just defeated the world's greatest superpower. They did it, by and large, with the weapons they had at home. The colonists were suffering under the oppression of an all-powerful central government in which they felt they had no representation. King George III ruled by official edict from London with total disregard for the popular opinions of the people.

Their taxes were raised and new taxes levied, and the Continental Congress filed grievances with the king. The Stamp Act again raised their taxes, and the Sons of Liberty were born. They protested this new tax and dumped tea into Boston Harbor. The event has gone down in history as the Boston Tea Party (occurring on my birthday, no point here other than I think that's cool). But none of those actions by the British were enough to cause the colonists to take up arms.

Then, on April 18, 1775, the British forces in Boston started marching to Concord. Their purpose was to seize the weapons and arms that the colonists had stored there. In the hearts and minds of the militiamen, that was the final straw. They would fight for their right to bear arms.

The first battles of the American Revolution were fought over the right of the private citizen to arm himself. Despite all the previous grievances the colonies had about taxes, fees, penalties, executive orders, and regulations it was the threat of the government to seize their arms that pushed the colonists to stop writing letters of grievances and start pulling triggers.

It was written as much to allow the private citizen to acquire arms as it was written to prevent a tyrannical central government from seizing the weapons the people already owned.

The Second Amendment is just as important now as it was then.

Opponents to the Second Amendment say that we no longer need weapons and that the personal ownership of firearms causes crime. That is statistically not at all true. In fact, the cities with the highest crime and murder rates are precisely those with the most stringent gun laws. Guns in the hands of a "well-regulated militia" are a threat to those who are bent on controlling a population. That is precisely why this is a right in the first place. It is a far better situation for We the People when the government fears us and we do not fear the government.

Additionally, if someone wanted to do his neighbor harm, he could do it with a rock, a garden rake, or a hammer. Not having a gun doesn't eliminate violence. Likewise, if my neighbor had no intention whatsoever of ever committing a violent crime, it wouldn't matter if he had a main battle tank in his garage.

As far as personal protection is concerned, you have an inherent God-given right to life. You have the inherent God-given right to protect the lives of your family and your property. That means you have the right to employ whatever means necessary to stop any threat you may face to protect your loved ones and your home up to and including deadly force. For the vast majority of cases, the police can only try to catch the guy that committed the crime. Very rarely are they present to prevent the crime in the first place. The Second Amendment exists for when seconds count and the police are minutes away.

**Third Amendment**: No Soldier shall, in time of peace be quartered in any house, without the consent of the Owner, nor in time of war, but in a manner to be prescribed by law.

The Third Amendment was ratified to protect the sanctity of the home from governmental intrusion. Our founder Samuel Adams summarizes the risk of not protecting the sanctity and inherent privacy of the American home from the military when he wrote the following:

> Soldiers are not gover'd properly by the laws of their country, but by a law made for them only. This may in time make them look upon themselves as a body of men different from the rest of the people; and as they and they only have the sword in their hands, they may sooner or later begin to look upon themselves as the LORDS and not the SERVANTS of the people: Instead of enforcing the execution of law,

> which by the way is far from being the original intent of Soldiers, they may refuse to obey it themselves, and enforce them by the power of the sword. (3)

The rule that the government can't put soldiers in your house should be pretty straightforward. However, with the militarization of our country's police forces, it has been argued that the line has been blurred. One of the chief arguments the colonists had with the British was that the people were being forced to house soldiers. There have now been several court cases stating that, in effect, if the police show up to your house with armored personnel carriers, body armor, helmets, stun grenades, and submachine guns, they are in effect soldiers.

For example, there was a case in Nevada where the police forcibly occupied a family's home because they wanted to "gain a tactical advantage" over the suspected criminals they were investigating who lived next door. The police came to the house, asked the couple who lived there, Michael and Linda Mitchell, if the SWAT team could occupy the house. The Mitchells were not suspected of any crime and the police didn't have a warrant. The Mitchells denied the police access to their home.

After that, according to the Mitchell's suit, things got ugly. The suit claims they then aimed their weapons, commanding him to lie down on the floor and crawl toward them. When he didn't move, they allegedly fired pepper-spray balls at him, striking him three times at close range and causing him to "experience uncontrollable coughing and difficulty breathing," the suit says. Police then arrested Mr. Mitchell for "obstructing a police officer" before "swarming" into his home. He also claims they fired pepper-balls at his cowering dog named Sam. (4)

The meat of the case is whether the state police take over a private home for their own purposes without a warrant and where the residents are not suspected of any crime. Is that fundamentally different than if the state placed a National Guard, a military unit, in the home? The federal judge ruled that it is different. The Mitchells lost their claim against the police.

I am generally in full support of our brave law enforcement officers who put their lives on the line for us every day. They have a very tough, dangerous and more often than not thankless job. The vast majority of police deserve our utmost respect and support. My great grandfather was a city policeman in my hometown. My mother's father was a county deputy sheriff and my father was a military policeman in Korea. I have a long family history in law enforcement. However, watching the videos of the police pulling law-abiding citizens from their homes at gunpoint, to include women and children, while looking for the suspects in the Boston Marathon bombing, I begin to question the motives and tactics of some of them, however small a minority that represents. This leads us straight to unlawful searches.

**Fourth Amendment**: The right of the people to be secure in their persons, houses, papers, and effects, against unreasonable searches and seizures, shall not be violated, and no Warrants shall issue, but upon probable cause, supported by Oath or affirmation, and particularly describing the place to be searched, and the persons or things to be seized.

Ever been stopped and interrogated by your state police at a drunk-driving police roadblock? Have you ever been driving down the road, minding your own business, and been stopped and interrogated, complete with a drug-sniffing dog circling your car, by the federal border patrol? Have you ever been walking down the sidewalk and been asked by a police officer to be "stopped and frisked" for no apparent reason? If you have experienced any of these incidents, did you feel secure in your person, or did you feel unreasonably searched?

The practice of "stop and frisk" has been upheld by the Supreme Court as not being in violation of the Fourth Amendment. But the Supreme Court also ruled that a black person was property and not a citizen in 1857. The Supreme Court ruled segregation was legal in 1896. The Supreme Court also ruled that the murder of unborn babies was legal in 1973. The fact that a majority of nine fallible and mortal people rule on a subject doesn't automatically make them right.

I can appreciate the narrative that stop and frisk prevents crime. I'm fully in favor of enforcing the little crimes to prevent the bigger ones, known as the "broken window" theory. Meaning that if you arrest the guy who breaks a window and fully enforce the law, we'll prevent burglaries, assaults, armed robberies, etc. My question is strictly is stop and frisk a violation of the individual's right to be secure in their person? As Supreme Court Justice William O. Douglas wrote in his dissenting opinion in the case of *Terry v. Ohio*, which is the case New York uses to legalize its policy of stop and frisk,

> Yet if the individual is no longer to be sovereign, if the police can pick him up whenever they do not like the cut of his jib, if they can "seize" and "search" him in their discretion, we enter a new regime. The decision to enter it should be made only after a full debate by the people of this country (https://www.law.cornell.edu/supremecourt/text/392/1).

Before the police or any other government agent can search you, your house, or your car they must present to a magistrate probable cause to believe you are either going to commit or in the process of committing a crime. Of course, there are exceptions when immediate steps are necessary to save lives or property.

We have a right to simply be left alone. We forfeit that right only if we infringe upon the rights of another citizen. In other words, if you're not pumping wastewater into your neighbor's yard, robbing a store, running a meth lab in your basement, or otherwise committing a crime, you should never fear the agents of the government coming to your home. There is an inherent right to privacy. Yes, that includes the National Security Agency (NSA) monitoring your phone calls or e-mails.

If the government believes you are committing a crime or are about to, they need to explain their case before a judge. Their case must include who you are, what they think you are doing, and where they think you are doing it. In their warrant, the government must also include what they are looking for when they come to your house. It isn't enough for them to just list the suspected crime. They have to state the items they are looking for in their search. To me, we are increasingly sacrificing our privacy. The founders would have never foreseen everyone being felt up by the TSA at the airports, for example.

There are ways for the government to violate our privacy other than with a battering ram at our front doors, too. With the government's implementation of Obamacare and Common Core, the government is data mining like never before. When we go to the doctor's office or when our kids are at school, we are being asked such things as what our political affiliation is, if there are guns in our houses, and even what religious beliefs we have. None of those things are any of the government's business. We need to collectively stand up for our rights and refuse to comply with these questions.

The city of Albany, New York, just passed a law that requires all guns to be locked up inside people's homes. The issue as to this law's potential for infringing on our rights really relates to its enforcement. With the passage of this law, coupled with the mandatory registration of all guns with the government, will the police now have carte blanche to enter the homes of gun owners under the auspices of checking to see if our guns are locked up? Won't that mean they can come in at any time without a warrant? All they have to do is print out the list of all local registered gun owners and go door to door. Other states, such as Delaware, have similar bills pending. I don't see how such laws—especially the enforcement of such laws—could possibly be constitutional.

**Fifth Amendment**: No person shall be held to answer for a capital, or otherwise infamous crime, unless on a presentment or indictment of a Grand Jury, except in cases arising in the land or naval forces, or in the Militia, when in actual service in time of War or public danger; nor shall any person be subject for the same offence to be twice put in jeopardy of life or limb; nor shall be compelled in any criminal case to be a witness against himself, nor be deprived of life, liberty, or property, without due process of law; nor shall private property be taken for public use, without just compensation.

You can't just be dragged out of your home unless and until you have been formally charged with a crime presented before a magistrate. The government must have an arrest warrant first unless police catch you in the process of committing a crime or have good reason to suspect you of having just done so. A street cop hears a lady screaming. He runs to the sound of her voice, and she tells him that someone just snatched her purse. Looking up, he sees someone carrying a purse sprinting from the scene. He can track down and arrest that person without going to a magistrate to seek an arrest warrant. Common sense.

For any crime, you can be tried only once. If you are found innocent, you can't be dragged off to another trial. If you are sure of either your innocence or that the law is unjust, request your constitutionally protected right of a trial by jury. Force the government to prove your guilt. If the law is unjust, use your time before your jury—and it is *your* jury, to inform them of their power of jury nullification (see final chapter).

The government can't make you testify against yourself. This is what is meant when a defendant "pleads the Fifth."

The clause concerning being "deprived of life, liberty, or property, without due process of law" can get murky, especially when it comes to the IRS. Even in cases with the IRS, you have the right to seek redress before a judge and jury. The problem is that the IRS is a huge and monstrous bureaucracy with enormous resources at its disposal to attack you and sees any and every attempt to legally avoid taxes as tax evasion. The true threats to our liberty are really abused due to the enormous IRS investigative powers backed by prosecutors of the US Justice Department. The IRS can simply seize your assets, garnish your wages or take your house to collect whatever they say you owe them.

Congressional hearings that were held a few years ago on the IRS publicly exposed what most Americans already knew: the IRS often conducts its affairs like a financial gestapo by trampling the rights of citizens. The IRS still views taxpayers as adversaries and assumes them to be guilty until they can prove otherwise. We are supposed to be assumed innocent until proven guilty. In cases where the government is in the process of seizing your property, when you are being crushed by the leviathan of the state, I assure you, it won't seem much like due process at all.

**Sixth Amendment**: In all criminal prosecutions, the accused shall enjoy the right to a speedy and public trial, by an impartial jury of the state and district wherein the crime shall have been committed, which district shall have been previously ascertained by law, and to be informed of the nature and cause of the accusation; to be confronted with the witnesses against him; to have compulsory process for obtaining witnesses in his favor, and to have the Assistance of Counsel for his defense.

Imagine being dragged out of your house and arrested. You're then stashed away in a dungeon somewhere, and no one tells you what you've done wrong. You languish there for years without a trial. When the trial does happen, it is behind closed doors and in secret. The state presents anonymous witnesses against you before a jury of representatives of the state who are obviously biased against you. You're also all alone with no lawyer or anyone else representing you. The Sixth Amendment exists to prevent all of these "holy crap!" situations from ever occurring against an American citizen.

This amendment guarantees defendants the right to a public trial before a jury of their peers without unnecessary delay. Who decides what constitutes unnecessary delay? Well, most states deem anything over one year too long. If you're not released on bail or bond, a year in jail waiting for a trial for a crime you didn't commit would definitely seem not speedy at all.

Both the defense and the prosecution can question potential jurors to help guarantee impartiality. In some cases, despite this amendment's provision that the trial be held in the district where the crime was committed, trials have been moved for various reasons.

**Seventh Amendment**: In suits at common law, where the value in controversy shall exceed twenty dollars, the right of trial by jury shall be preserved, and no fact tried by a jury, shall be otherwise reexamined in any court of the United States, than according to the rules of the common law.

The Seventh Amendment guarantees your right to request a trial by jury in federal court for civil cases. If you have been wronged and seek compensation from another citizen, to include companies and corporations, you have a right to plead your case before a jury of your peers. Despite the depreciated value of the original twenty dollars, that is still the legal threshold to bring your case before a jury if a federal court holds jurisdiction. Most states have adopted the standards of the Seventh Amendment for state jurisdiction as well.

**Eighth Amendment**: Excessive bail shall not be required, nor excessive fines imposed, nor cruel and unusual punishments inflicted.

The real question here is who determines what is excessive in terms of both bail and fines? When there are no victims or property damage and you are fined $185 for a traffic ticket, is that excessive? In most cases of the local courts, you will receive a speeding ticket for going a few miles over the posted limit. Of course, in respect to your Constitution, you are innocent. It is incumbent upon the court, the government, to prove your guilt. Most often, that's not what happens. To avoid the trouble, most people simply plead guilty on the ticket and mail it in to the court.

I use this example because most of us will never be charged with capital murder or counterfeiting. If we have any run-ins with the law and the courts, it will generally be for minor traffic offenses and the like.

If you do go to court at the appointed time, you likely will never see a judge. Instead, your district attorney's office will send down the junior assistant deputy vice district attorney to offer you a plea deal. The state will do just about everything possible to avoid your going to anything that resembles an actual trial before a jury of your peers. Those are expensive to the state and eat up a lot of time. The state doesn't want it. Instead, this lackey from the district attorney's office will offer you a lesser charge and try to convince you to plead guilty to that. I've personally received a few speeding tickets, and I've been consistently offered deals such as pleading guilty to "failure to obey a traffic control device" and "parking in an illegal zone" instead of speeding.

Accepting the lesser charge might avoid points on your license and your rates being jacked up on your car insurance, but it doesn't avoid the monetary charges the state will impose. Your fine might be less, but the court charges and fees make up the difference. Even with a $25 fine, you're not walking out of there, regardless of the charge, for less than $150 with the added court costs and fees. Is that excessive? Who decides? Technically, it's not a fine. Let's be honest; tickets and these types of charges are more about generating revenue for the jurisdiction than about dispensing any kind of justice.

As far as "cruel and unusual punishment" goes, our Framers and Supreme Court cases since both judged there would be "evolving standards of decency" that would define what the words cruel and unusual mean. For instance, it is unconstitutional to execute criminals who have committed murder if they killed while they were still minors. It is cruel and unusual for prison guards to beat prisoners. But it is not cruel or unusual if the state attempts to electrocute a convicted murderer, fails, and then tries again four weeks after the first attempt, as has happened before and was upheld by the courts as not being cruel or unusual.

**Ninth Amendment**: The enumeration in the Constitution, of certain rights, shall not be construed to deny or disparage others retained by the people.

This means the fact that other rights may not appear in the Constitution doesn't mean they aren't our rights. We the people are assumed to be free. We the people created government to perform a certain number of functions on our behalf. The Constitution doesn't apply to us. It is a list of limited powers we grant to government, at the consent of the governed. If we feel the government is out of control, we retain the right to amend or abolish it. We own government, not the other way around. Unfortunately those we have elected to represent us in government seem to have taken the attitude that they rule over us. The way the system has been built up since then, these people kind of do rule over us. They need a reminder of just how wrong they are.

We the people are supreme. We rule over Washington, our state capitals, our town halls, and even our courts. For example, and I'll cover this in greater depth later, a jury of citizens in a courtroom can legally decide that a law or a judge's opinion is unjust, illegal, or just wrong. A jury can decide that a punishment for any given crime is excessive. A jury can legally and unquestionably nullify both law and legal decisions. We the people are the final arbiters. We rule.

**Tenth Amendment**: The powers not delegated to the United States by the Constitution, nor prohibited by it to the states, are reserved to the states respectively, or to the people.

The federal government has the powers listed here in the Constitution and *only* those powers. If it isn't in the Constitution as a specific power to the federal government, the federal government can't do it. Period.

There are many other things the people may decide they want the federal government to do, but without adding an amendment to the Constitution, the government cannot legally do it. That doesn't mean your state or local governments can't act on those issues. It is just that the *federal* government doesn't have that power.

That isn't to say that our federal government doesn't have power, of course it does and it should. The Framers of the Constitution gave our federal government just enough power to do the things it is supposed to be doing, and not much more. Everything else is left to either the state governments to do, or to We the People.

As it is today, the federal government seems to do whatever it wants. It either just passes the law, like the Affordable Care Act, regardless if healthcare is in the Constitution or not or it relies on the huge government bureaucracy to assume the power under some regulation. It doesn't matter what is or is not listed in the supreme law of the land, the Constitution, as a power of government. It just does whatever it wants. It will keep right on doing it too, unless we stop them.

What are these enumerated powers of government? I'm glad you asked.

# 8

## The Powers of Government

**With respect to the words general welfare, I have always regarded them as qualified by the detail of powers connected with them. To take them in a literal and unlimited sense would be a metamorphosis of the Constitution into a character which there is a host of proofs was not contemplated by its creators.**

— James Madison

The US Constitution defined what powers the government would possess. These listed eighteen items are the *only* items upon which the federal government could legislate; nothing more. It should be noted here that all federal officials, the president on down, judges, senators, representatives, and even newly inducted members of the armed forces, take an oath to support and defend the Constitution "against all enemies, foreign and domestic." The oath isn't to the president or a party.

I know the government today does so much more than the items listed here. Those "extra" things the federal government controls are all unconstitutional. All of them. That includes such things as social security, Medicare, food stamps, welfare, Pell grants, and the like.

I know what you're thinking: "Wait, we need all those federal programs! Without them, people would starve, wouldn't have any income in their old age, and couldn't go to college. Just how heartless *are* you to want to cancel all of those programs for the needy?"

First, just because something may or may not be needed does not make it a power of the *federal* government. Think of the layers of government between you and Washington, DC. You have your town hall, county, and state governments that could run many of these programs, if the voters of that jurisdiction decided the issue at hand is important enough to spend their collective tax dollars on. Who knows the needs of your community better than the people of your community? Does an unelected bureaucrat hundreds or thousands of miles away know the needs of your town better than the elected members of your town council? I sincerely doubt it.

"But wait," you may say. "The federal government has *way* more money than my town, county, or state does. Where would we get the money to administer these programs?"

Well, to start with, big governments are expensive, and it takes a really big government to try to provide everything to everyone all the time. For example, the operating budget of the Department of Education is $77.4 billion and forty-four hundred employees. That's $77,400,000,000 to run a department that there is no mention of anywhere in the Constitution.

The Social Security Administration has sixty-six thousand employees and an annual operating budget of $16.4 billion, yet there is no provision for social security in the Constitution. So just eliminating those two unconstitutional departments would return $93,800,000,000 to the pockets of the American taxpayers. There are hundreds of such examples.

The natural tendency of all government agencies is to grow in budget, size, and control. That is true for all levels of government. I was once a county government department head in northern New York. The county was facing a budget shortfall at the time, and the department heads were tasked with finding some savings in their budgets and presenting them to the legislature. Instead, almost across the board, the departments came one by one before the legislature to explain why there wasn't any money to be saved anywhere in their respective budgets and how they instead really needed and deserved more money. That happened all the time. Departments would routinely come before the board asking for more funding to expand their departments, hire more employees, get another office or boardroom, and so on, which, of course, cost more money—our money.

If the federal government suddenly wanted to act responsibly and initiate a federal department of budget reform and government savings, in no time flat that agency would have ten thousand unionized employees and cost us $25 billion per year to run.

There are so many laws, rules, and regulations that Americans routinely break three laws a day without even knowing it. Let that sink in for a moment. There are just too many laws. We really can't say we are free.

James Madison emphasized these points when he wrote the following:

> It will be of little avail to the people that the laws are made by men of their own choice if the laws be so voluminous that they cannot be read, or so incoherent that they cannot be understood; if they be repealed or revised before they are promulgated, or undergo such incessant changes that no man, who knows what the law is today, can guess what it will be tomorrow. Law is defined to be a rule of action; but how can that be a rule, which is little known and less fixed? (1)

Speaking of voluminous laws, just this last week on 18 December, 2015, Congress just passed the 2016 Ominbus Spending Bill. This one law which covers more than $1 trillion in spending of taxpayer dollars was 2009 pages long. It was presented to our representatives and Senators less than 48 hours before they were expected to vote on it. Of course, no one had time to actually read the bill and fully understand what they were voting on. (2)

If we the people held the federal government to the powers listed in the Constitution and only the powers listed in the Constitution, we would save hundreds of dollars every year. In addition, this would greatly limit the power and scope of the federal government and that of its departments, agencies, and bureaus that are filled with a veritable army of unelected bureaucrats, lawyers, and judges who now collectively control nearly every aspect of our lives. There are now more people working for government in America than are employed in manufacturing. Doesn't anyone else see how wrong this is? It is high time we return power back to the states and our local governments, exactly where it belongs.

Would you rather have most of the laws and regulations that impact you, your family, and your property come from the Washington, DC, or from your town hall? If they come from your town hall, you can walk down there for the board meetings and let them have it. I believe at least 90 percent of all our governance should come from people you know by name and can easily toss out of office and replace if needed.

Public service should be just that—service. Citizens should be chosen and should reluctantly leave their businesses, jobs, or farms for a designated period of time to go serve. They do their duty, go home, and let the next guy or gal take their place. There is no place in a true representative republic for career politicians.

If you disagree with something going on in Washington, you're left to write a letter or make a phone call—or, as it practically happens, you're left frustrated and powerless. Let's be honest for a moment. The people in Washington really don't care what sign you hold over your head, what march you take part in, or which petition you sign online. They're going to do whatever they like. In practical terms, you don't matter.

That attitude isn't limited to our federal government, either. For example, on January 15, 2013, the SAFE Act was passed in New York. The new law required the registration of existing "assault rifles" and banned the sale of new ones in New York, banned more than seven bullets in a magazine of any firearm, and added many other restrictions on the private ownership of firearms. By any reasonable standard, this law is a clear violation of the Second

Amendment. There was an immediate outcry not only against the law itself but against the way it was passed. Governor Andrew Cuomo and the legislature violated the New York state constitution rules when the bill was pushed through in the middle of the night and it was signed into law the next day.

Since the SAFE Act became law, there have been marches, protests, and rallies calling for its repeal. Fifty-two of sixty-two counties have passed legislation also calling for the law's repeal. One of the provisions of the law is that all "assault weapons" must be registered with New York state. Of the estimated one million such weapons in the state, only forty-five thousand have been registered. That is a compliance rate of about 4.5 percent, meaning that just about 95 percent of all gun owners in the state of New York decided to not comply with this unconstitutional law.

All of that has not made one bit of difference. The law still stands. The moral of the story is that those in power simply do not care what we think. They don't care what our values are or what we feel is important. They don't care if they infringe on our rights or not. They don't even, generally speaking, know or care what our rights are or acknowledge that it is their job to protect those rights.

It all comes down to the value of the individual. Are our rights truly endowed upon us by our Creator and therefore unalienable, or is our freedom subject to the whims of government officials, elected and unelected? Our rights and freedoms existed before any government existed. They are ours, and government exists at our consent, not the other way around. Our rights came from our Creator and only our Creator can take them.

We'll quickly go through the list of the enumerated powers of the federal government. Become familiar with these. Anything and everything else that the federal government has its fingers in is unconstitutional—that is, illegal.

Enumerated powers of the federal government:

1. The Congress shall have Power To lay and collect Taxes, Duties, Imposts and Excises, to pay the Debts and provide for the common Defence and general Welfare of the United States; but all Duties, Imposts and Excises shall be uniform throughout the United States;

It is important to note here that this first enumerated power is "to lay and collect taxes, duties, imposts, and excises." General welfare is *not* a separate enumerated power. If it were, the government could do just about anything to us and use the excuse that "it's for the general welfare." This clause has been misused and misapplied more than any other part of the Constitution.

2. To borrow Money on the credit of the United States;

The government has the exercise of this power down to a science. It has to borrow just about 40 percent of all the money it spends. Our founders knew the risk of allowing the government to borrow too much. Thomas Jefferson warned against this and thought it immoral for one generation to pass federal debt to the next, writing, "We shall all consider ourselves unauthorized to saddle posterity with our debts, and morally bound to pay them ourselves; and consequently within what may be deemed the period of a generation, or the life [expectancy] of the majority." (3)

Up until the twentieth century, every government strived to eliminate debt from our treasury. We have carried a national debt since the Great Depression. In essence, we are still paying off the bills that President Roosevelt put on the books.

For at least the last 100 years or so, we have been borrowing money to pay for the expansion of the federal government at an ever increasing rate. This translates into generational theft as we write IOUs our children and grandchildren will be left to pay. This has to end.

As of 13 January, 2016, the national debt was $18,896,531,182,152.07 and grows every single day by about $2,360,000,000.00! (4) How can any elected representative morally continue to spend at such a rate knowing full well that this generation will never be able to pay this off?

3. To regulate Commerce with foreign Nations, and among the several States, and with the Indian Tribes;

At the time of the framing of the Constitution, "to regulate" meant to make regular, or uniform. This enumerated power wasn't supposed to be a blank check for the government to write thousands and thousands of regulations every year, year in and year out. It was meant to ensure that New Jersey couldn't impose a tariff on oak barrels coming in from New York. This power has been insanely misinterpreted and abused.

4. To establish an uniform Rule of Naturalization, and uniform Laws on the subject of Bankruptcies throughout the United States;

There has been a lot of discussion lately on immigration, legal and illegal. The president, the Department of Justice, the attorney general, and others fall within the category of those who cannot abridge, change, or choose to enforce or not enforce the laws concerning naturalization. This power is specifically given only to Congress. Any other presidential edict, executive order, nullification, selective enforcement rule, or anything else is unconstitutional and, therefore, null and void.

5. To coin Money, regulate the Value thereof, and of foreign Coin, and fix the Standard of Weights and Measures;

There was a time when each state printed and coined its own money. Even companies had their own script used as currency. It was a mess. This fixed that.

6. To provide for the Punishment of counterfeiting the Securities and current Coin of the United States;

Counterfeiting American money is a federal crime. The Secret Service is the policing agency tasked with catching counterfeiters.

7. To establish Post Offices and post Roads;

The federal highway system is an enumerated power of the federal government. There is a national gasoline tax on every gallon of fuel we put in our cars and trucks that is earmarked to upkeep the roads. They always spend more. Worse, our representatives use the annual highway bill to get as much pork for their respective districts as possible. A new bridge means jobs. Jobs mean reelection. The annual highway bill, in addition to actually funding many or few actual needed improvements and repairs to our infrastructure, has become a huge pork spending program so the folks in Congress can say, "Look how great I am! I got you all this federal money! Reelect me!" In short, federal highway money is used to buy votes as much as to fix our roads and bridges.

8. To promote the Progress of Science and useful Arts, by securing for limited Times to Authors and Inventors the exclusive Right to their respective Writings and Discoveries;

Here is another abused power. The power isn't "to promote the progress of science and useful arts." We shouldn't have a National Endowment of the Arts. That is unconstitutional. The federal government should never be giving our property away, in the form of tax revenue, to any artist for any purpose—including to Big Bird and National Public Radio.

The power here is to secure exclusive right to one's writings and discoveries. Or, in other words, to grant patents. That's it. The federal government can grant patents—which are extremely important to protect personal property rights and the intellectual property of inventors, writers, and entrepreneurs—but there is no constitutional provision for the US taxpayer to fund the arts. Once it does, we have bureaucrats defining what is and what is not aesthetically worthwhile and therefore worthy of plundering the national coffers to support.

The marketplace is a much better determinant of what is and what is not worthy of being called art. If a play is a good one, people will buy tickets to see it. If an artist has talent and his paintings are beautiful, people will buy them. Government just distorts all this, opening the door to corruption.

9. To constitute Tribunals inferior to the Supreme Court;

Congress establishes lower federal courts. That means Congress can abolish lower federal courts. Not the Supreme Court; that is a separate branch of government. But the lower courts owe their existence to Congress. If a lower federal court makes what Congress deems an unconstitutional ruling, Congress can repeal that court's charter and force it to close. Any truly representative body whose charter was to uphold and defend the Constitution to guarantee the rights of the citizens would do just that. It would keep doing it, too, until the federal courts got it in their heads that their only job is to also uphold the Constitution and defend the rights of the citizens.

10. To define and punish Piracies and Felonies committed on the high Seas, and Offences against the Law of Nations;

There has been a lot of criticism against the president from his detractors regarding his negligence in naming our enemies in the Middle East—namely, ISIS and other Islamic terrorist groups. The constitutional power to legally name the enemies of the United States lies with Congress.

At the time of the Framers, the piracies to be defined lay in the Islamic Barbary Pirates coming out of modern-day Libya. In the time of muskets and sailing ships, the Barbary Pirates were terrorists. Today, Congress can steer the national debate and formally declare—or in constitutional terms, define—our enemies through resolution. They haven't done so and show no signs of doing so. Honestly, they'd rather point fingers and get their sound bites on TV than do their jobs as defined by the Constitution that each member swore to uphold. What does it mean to us as a nation when our elected representatives would rather fix blame than fix our problems?

11. To declare War, grant Letters of Marque and Reprisal, and make Rules concerning Captures on Land and Water;

Congress and only Congress has the power to declare war. The last time this happened was World War II. Every conflict since has been without a formal, legal declaration of war. Of course, as commander in chief of the armed forces, the president has the authority to act and employ our military in times of emergency. But I believe that if our American sons and daughters are going to be put in harm's way for any extended period of time, it needs to be for a declared war.

Not only would our representatives have the opportunity to debate whether any particular conflict is worth expending our greatest treasure, our servicemen and women, but it would also place a national emphasis on the conflict. Right now we are essentially at war. We still have our people fighting and dying in Afghanistan. If you were to drive around or watch the news, you'd never know it. Each time I came back from a combat tour in Iraq, after the welcome home ceremonies, once I left the base, you'd never guess we were a nation at war. A formal declaration of war by Congress might focus the American psyche on the conflict and make defeating our enemies a national endeavor, just as it should be.

12. To raise and support Armies, but no Appropriation of Money to that Use shall be for a longer Term than two Years;
13. To provide and maintain a Navy;
14. To make Rules for the Government and Regulation of the land and naval Forces;

People often complain about the amount of money the government spends on the military, and that's fine. In a representative republic with at least a semblance of a freedom of speech, complaining about the government is ok. But usually there isn't much of a complaint about the hundreds if not thousands of other things the government is spending money on that aren't in the Constitution at all. At least raising and supporting armies and providing and maintaining a navy are in the Constitution.

But that doesn't stop politicians from using federal funding of our national defense for their own purposes. I live right outside Fort Drum, New York, home of the 10th Mountain light infantry division with which I have proudly served. Every election year, every politician from local, state, and national office is guaranteed to come up here and say, "If you vote for me, I will save Fort Drum." Then, like some self-fulfilling prophecy, when Fort Drum isn't closed, they come back around at election time with "Look, I saved Fort Drum!" Never mind that Fort Drum was never at risk of closing anyway.

While we're on the subject of national defense, let me add a quick note here. There is truth behind Ronald Reagan's philosophy of "peace through strength." Even our founders knew this. Benjamin Franklin wrote on the subject:

> Our security lies, I think, in our growing strength, both in numbers and wealth; that creates an increasing ability of assisting this nation in its wars, which will make us more respectable, our friendship more valued, and our enmity feared; thence it will soon be thought proper to treat us not with justice only, but with kindness, and thence we may expect in a few years a total change of measures with regard to us; unless, by a neglect of military discipline, we should lose all martial spirit, and our western people become as tame as those in the eastern dominions of Britain [India], when we may expect the same oppressions; for there is much truth in the Italian saying, "Make yourselves sheep, and the wolves will eat you." (5)

Every time it seems America becomes pacifistic or isolationist, we are dragged into another war. It happened when we had the pacifist Woodrow Wilson in the White House and at World War I. Following that "war to end all wars," we disarmed only to have World War II a generation later. Now we have the smallest army since 1940 and are continuing to weaken our military. We have the Chinese navy patrolling in the Aleutian Islands and Russian intelligence trawlers off the coast of Georgia. I sincerely hope history doesn't repeat itself.

We have to possess the moral foundation to actually stand for something as a nation. Having a large and capable military comes with the responsibility to use it sparingly, in accordance with not only the Constitution, but with our national values and convictions.

15. To provide for calling forth the Militia to execute the Laws of the Union, suppress Insurrections and repel Invasions;
16. To provide for organizing, arming, and disciplining, the Militia, and for governing such Part of them as may be employed in the Service of the United States, reserving to the states respectively, the Appointment of the Officers, and the Authority of training the Militia according to the discipline prescribed by Congress;

These last two allow for the Congress to federalize the states' national guard forces in times of national crisis, during war, and in the event that Canada invades New Hampshire. Notice that the president can't do it, only Congress.

17. To exercise exclusive Legislation in all Cases whatsoever, over such District (not exceeding ten Miles square) as may, by Cession of particular States, and the Acceptance of Congress, become the Seat of the Government of the United States, and to exercise like Authority over all Places purchased by the Consent of the Legislature of the state in which the Same shall be, for the Erection of Forts, Magazines, Arsenals, dock-Yards, and other needful Buildings;

There is no provision in the Constitution for the federal government to possess the absolutely obscene swaths of land that it owns within the states. The only land specifically mentioned in the Constitution is the District of Columbia, not to exceed ten square miles.

According to a 2012 congressional research service report, the federal government owns roughly 635 million acres of land. I'm no mathematician, but I'm pretty sure that exceeds ten square miles.

For example, the federal government owns more than a third of Montana, Colorado, and New Mexico. It owns 42 percent of Arizona, 47 percent of California, nearly half of Wyoming, 53 percent of Washington, 62 percent of Idaho and Alaska, 67 percent of Utah, and 81 percent of Nevada. So much for state sovereignty (http://www.deseretnews.com/top/2318/43/

Arizona-From-03-to-811-What-percentage-of-each-state-is-owned-by-the-federal-government.html).

Yes, the federal government needs to own land for military bases, and it does. However, all the military bases in the country combined don't come close to the amount of all the other land the federal government controls. Why?

> 18. To make all Laws which shall be necessary and proper for carrying into Execution the foregoing Powers, and all other Powers vested by this Constitution in the Government of the United States, or in any Department or Officer thereof.

This means that if Congress needs to pass a law to carry out one of the other seventeen specific powers listed here, it can do that. This isn't a blank check for Congress to pass laws on anything else it may want to do. The powers of the federal government are still limited to only these eighteen specific enumerated powers. That's it. No more. Can't do it, unconstitutional. Everything else that the government has its fingers in is illegal.

Where is social security? Not here. Doesn't exist. Where is education? Not here either. Doesn't exist. The Department of Education and the Social Security Administration are unconstitutional. Where are welfare and the Environmental Protection Agency? Wow, they're not here either. So all of those programs and the huge bureaucratic agencies instituted to manage them are unconstitutional, too. Go figure.

We're talking about this because liberty is a zero-sum game. Either a right belongs to the people or it becomes a power of government. There is no middle ground. Every power assumed by government means less freedom left for "we the people." And by the way, governments do not have rights. The police do not have the right to search your house. They don't have any rights at all. Government only has power. It is only supposed to have the power that we by mutual consent allow. Period. That's why we have a Bill of Rights. We have a Bill of Rights to protect us from ourselves because we are mortal, fallible human beings.

The more distance between the people and those who exercise power, the more likely it is that our politicians and unelected bureaucrats are corrupt. Just as it is important for the citizens to personally know the people who are passing the laws that have the greatest impact on their lives, it should also be imperative for those legislators to know the people who will be affected by the laws they pass. It should go without saying that the people who are passing the laws should be subject to those same laws.

Today that is not the case at all. The Affordable Care Act comes immediately to mind. Congress wrote their own exemption into the law so they would never personally feel any of the negative effects from that piece of legislation of more than two thousand pages. But it goes far beyond that.

> In the House of Representatives there is not the substance, but the shadow only, of representation, which can never produce proper information in the legislature, or inspire confidence in the people. The laws will, therefore, be generally made by men little concerned in, and unacquainted with, their effects and consequences.
>
> —George Mason in objecting to the Constitution without a Bill of Rights, 1787

As it is, there has been such a vacuum in Washington just sucking up the power from every facet of our lives and at the expense of every level of government between the individual citizen and "them." That distance on a map creates an emotional distance in resonance and reason. To the lawmakers in Washington, exercising power over our lives and legislating on things never conceived of in the Constitution, we the people can become the rabble or—how they often refer to us—"the American people." We are no longer the American person. This is especially the case the longer they are up there. Our representatives become insulated from the laws they are passing. They don't ever see the effects of the legislation and really don't personally know anyone who has to suffer under their laws and regulations.

"Political power automatically gravitates toward the center," explains W. Cleon Skousen in his work, *The 5,000 Year Leap, 28 Great Ideas That Changed the World.* He added this:

> And the purpose of the Constitution is to prevent that from happening. The centralization of political power always destroys liberty by removing the decision-making function from the people on the local level and transferring it to the officers of the central government. This process gradually benumbs the spirit of "voluntarism" among the people, and they lose the will to solve their own problems. They also cease to be involved in community affairs. They seek the anonymity of oblivion in the seething crowds of the city and often degenerate into faceless automatons who have neither a voice nor a vote. (6)

The Framers of the US Constitution knew that it was an imperfect document at the time of its signing. Therefore, they included Article V, which stipulates the conditions for amending the Constitution. The process for making changes was intentionally hard. Amendments and changes to the framework by which our federal representative government operates should be not executed lightly and should be preceded by much debate and forethought.

But the Constitution has been changed, and there are so far twenty-seven amendments to the Constitution, so the process works.

The original founders were for a form of government in which the federal government would have limited powers and the states would retain their sovereignty. Their vision held that there would be two houses of Congress, one in which the people would be represented directly and the other where the interests of the states would be protected.

The members of the House of Representatives would be elected by the people and would hold the office for a term of two years. This was the people's House. With such a short term, the representatives would be most accountable to their constituents. If they acted in a manner that was contrary to the will of the people they represented, they would be replaced in two years.

The Senate was to represent the interest of the states. The federal government was created by the states and the people. The founders were worried that there would be a concentration of power under the federal government. One check to that power was the US Senate. There, the senators were chosen by the state legislatures so when they arrived in Washington, they would not represent the federal government but instead would fight for the interest of their state. If they acted in a manner that was contrary to the will of their state government, they could be recalled.

Today, debates about bailing out Wall Street or approval of the Keystone XL pipeline would be dramatically different if the senate were controlled by the states and not the leviathan that the federal government has become. States that would have seen jobs created for the pipeline construction and decreased oil costs due to increased supply would have lobbied hard for the pipeline.

The Affordable Care Act, or Obamacare, most likely would not have passed through the Senate if it mandated increased costs to the states for Medicare or Medicaid. The senators who represented the interest of the states and not the federal government would have blocked its passage.

The XVII Amendment changed the way senators are chosen. It took the power away from the states and concentrated it under the federal government. Some say that it was a move to a more democratic government now that the people choose their own senators. But it was a move by the Left-leaning progressive presidents, Taft and Woodrow Wilson, to concentrate power under the federal government at the expense of the states. These were the same administrations that imposed the first taxes on incomes as well.

We should repeal the XVII Amendment and deliver the power back to the states. This would dramatically change the paradigm of the debate at the federal level of every issue. The states would have a voice at the federal level again. That would entirely change the system, and no longer would the senators be beholden to party. No longer would senators such as Harry Reid be able to kill legislation that would benefit the states in the name of partisan politics. This would kill unfunded federal mandates to the states and protect the Tenth Amendment. This is a change that is long overdue.

State sovereignty is protected in the US Constitution in Article V and in the Tenth Amendment.

The Senate was intended to be a check on federal power. The recent actions of the federal government by executive edict, such as the Affordable Care Act, which mandates that churches provide contraception services against their faith, means there apparently are no functional checks to federal power. The debates in Congress and with the president are exclusively on what the effects of a particular piece of legislation may have, never on whether the federal government should be taking the action at all.

Among the clamor and confusion of partisan politics, government overreach, and out-of-control spending, the built-in safeguards that once protected the interests of the states—and, to a large extent, the people—are gone. The Repeal Amendment is a step in the right direction. The Repeal Amendment stipulates that states can opt out of any federal law that two-thirds of the states reject. This is an effort to restore federalism. Federalism is exactly what the appointment of senators by the state legislatures was designed to protect.

Our federal government is currently over $18 trillion in debt, and that doesn't take into account unfunded future liabilities. Congress passes laws and makes projections for cutting spending in the future and usually these projections go out ten years. The problem with that is there will be a different presidential administration and a different Congress in place in ten years. Congress can't make spending cuts or appropriations that a future Congress will be bound to. Additionally, the term "spending cuts" in Washington-speak has come to mean proposed reductions in future increases in spending, not real reductions in current spending.

So in the meantime, our debt increases at unprecedented levels, and no one in Washington is serious about making the necessary cuts to bring some fiscal responsibility to government. The states are without a voice at the federal level that could go a long way toward protecting us, "we the people."

We have representatives making careers out of two-year terms. There are many senators and representatives who have been in Washington for thirty, forty, and even fifty years! How in the world can they say they even identify, let alone truly represent, their districts when they haven't been one of us for their entire adult lives? We have representatives in both houses who have never had a single private sector job their entire lives. They went from college to congressional staff to elected office. Yet these people are passing laws every day that affect the lives of business people, farmers, fisheries, and restaurants where they've never had to work. They have no idea what they are doing, and they don't care, just as long as they get reelected.

Their kids will never eat the school lunches mandated by Washington because their kids go to private schools. They won't see the effects their massive comprehensive laws have on small business owners because they don't and probably never will own or try to run a small business. By and large, we've created an elite class that hangs out together, rubs elbows at cocktail parties hosted by corporate lobbyists, plays golf together, and really never has to see us, the masses. At election time, they pull the tattered list of promises out of their pockets for stump speeches to spew to us and convince us to vote for them. Once they get reelected—and they do, more than 95 percent of the time—they go back to Washington. Nothing changes.

The entire concept of public service is foreign to the vast majority of our representatives. The relationship between the citizen and our government has been turned upside down. It was supposed to be that we the people created a government to perform a specific list of duties on our behalf. They worked for us. Those chosen to represent us did so as a public trust and public service. They did their civic duty and came home and made room for the next person. Boy, have things changed.

It isn't just our elected representatives. When we allow our federal government rule over us on every issue from preschool to buying a house to planning for our retirement and everything in between, it doesn't take long for our unelected bureaucrats to become physically and mentally detached from the rules and regulations they are imposing on us. For example, we can have a bureaucrat from urban Connecticut working at the EPA writing regulations that define fines and penalties that will hit farmers in California and Wyoming. And these regulations carry the force of law, sometimes including possible prison sentences. But the bureaucrat sitting behind his desk in DC will never meet or know these people whose lives will be turned upside down because of what he does every day for his job. These people have no value to him. His union job is secure. He'll faithfully do his twenty years in his cubicle, will collect his pension, and will never have to answer for any of the rules and regulations he was paid to blindly impose on us. The entire army of unelected bureaucrats, over two million of them, is busy every day either writing regulations or enforcing them with hardly any personal accountability for the absolute beating we are taking down here on Main Street.

That's why it is so important that the lawmakers and the people under those laws know each other. That's why the federal government was limited to eighteen specific powers over which it could legislate. Everything else was left to the states and to "we the people." If we had adhered to the Constitution, the day-to-day operations and laws of the federal government would be just about inconsequential in our lives, just as they should be.

The rabble has no intrinsic individual value; however, if our real governance came not from Washington but from our town hall, the rabble would turn into Mr. and Mrs. Smith. The new second-grade math curriculum being voted on by your town council would be taught to their kids by your aunt Sylvia. We become real people again. We have value. That is exactly how our representative republic was designed to be.

People easily become corrupted by power, money, and control. Once they have it—whether president, speaker of the house, or county department head—not only will they fight to keep it, but they almost invariably want more. Power can be very intoxicating. You're elected to office, and suddenly overnight it seems everyone is vying for your attention and offering you this or that to curry your favors. Often these people suddenly think they are above the law. As with the woman sitting behind the desk at the Baghdad Council of Ministers, the focus can shift from "How can I help you" to "Want to get upstairs? Pay me."

Another problem is that we often judge the performance of our representatives not by how well they upheld their oath to uphold the Constitution and their oath of office. We no longer judge them on how well they protected the rights of the individual citizen or were good stewards of public funds or their public trust. No, now our elected representatives—especially at the federal level, but at the state level, too—are usually judged solely on how much money they can get for projects in their representative districts. That was never their job! But if they can get a bridge built or funding for a new school or whatever else, they're suddenly heroes. It doesn't matter if they destroy the rest of the country in the process. If we reward our representatives who are making forty-year careers out of two-year terms with reelection based on how well they can plunder the national treasury on our behalf, what do you think they will focus on while in Washington?

Such a power vacuum leading to Washington perpetrates a general feeling of either utter helplessness or disconnection to politics by the individual citizen. There is a widespread feeling now in America that "it doesn't matter; there's nothing I can do about it anyway." That is not only sad but also pretty close to true. People unplug. They can't do anything about it anyway, so they quit paying attention. Over time, the entire concept of government, governance, and civics has changed in this country.

If you ask someone to say the first thing they think of when you say "government," they're much more likely to say the president or Congress than their mayor or their own city council.

That's a problem in itself. Nothing empowers a corrupt government more than a disconnected and apathetic polis. If they can perpetuate the mind-set that the people's vote doesn't matter, those in Washington can continue to do whatever they like and continue to get reelected, and they do. Even when Congress has an overall approval rating in the single digits, people by and large still like their own representative. So who do they think is responsible?

That is when the states really have to stand up. The states were supposed to be the guardians protecting "we the people" from a centralized government that could very easily become tyrannical. The system we have emphasizes the separation of powers. Not only between the three branches of the federal government but also between the federal government and the individual states. The Framers had to reassure the states that the federal government would not become too powerful. Again, both liberty and power are zero-sum games. One branch of government cannot assume a responsibility or power without either seizing that power from another branch of government or trampling the people's liberty.

When the Constitution was first drafted, the states were very reluctant to sign on in support. They were justifiably worried that the new central government would become supreme and crush the states' role in governing. To allay those fears, our Framers wrote the Federalist Papers. Interestingly, at least to me, the Federalist Papers were first written to my home state of New York, but were later distributed around the country. In Federalist 45, James Madison wrote to address the issue of whether the federal government would in the end take for itself so much power as to render the states insignificant:

> The component parts of the state governments will in no instance be indebted for their appointment to the direct agency of the federal government, and very little, if at all, to the local influence of its members. The number of individuals employed under the Constitution of the United States will be much smaller than the number employed under the particular States. There will consequently be less of personal influence on the side of the former than of the latter. The members of the legislative, executive, and judiciary departments of thirteen and more States, the justices of peace, officers of militia, ministerial officers of justice, with all the county, corporation, and town officers, for three million and more of people, intermixed, and having particular acquaintance with every class and circle of people, must exceed, beyond all proportion, both in number and influence, those of every description who will be employed in the administration of the federal system. (4)

By design, the states were to do more and be more involved in the citizens' day-to-day lives than the federal government. That's how the rule book is written. Now the states have taken on more of a role of being the executors of federal policy than of being the primary governing body in the country. There are several ways the feds get the states to play along. First, Congress would just pass laws that the states would have to pay to execute. Called unfunded mandates, these were supposed to be at least reduced by the Unfunded Mandate Reform Act passed in 1995. The feds still do it, but it is less than before.

According to a study conducted by the United States Conference of Mayors in June 2005 titled "Impact of Unfunded Federal Mandates and Cost Shifts to US Cities, these costs are exorbitant.

"In 1993, The U.S. Conference of Mayors published the first national study of the impact of unfunded federal mandates on U.S. cities. The survey of cities conducted at that time found that a sample of 10 unfunded mandates cost all cities an estimated $6.5 billion in 1993 and would cost an estimated $54 billion over five years –a significant portion of cities' annual budgets over that period." (5)

The other way the federal government gets the states to do its bidding is through bribery and extortion. Remember the gas shortages when Jimmy Carter was president? Suddenly, the president wanted everyone to use less gasoline. One of the steps the government took to force us to do that was to lower the speed limit to 55 mph. Wait, the federal government has no constitutional power over speed limits, right? No, it doesn't. To force its will on the states, the feds simply told the states that to receive federal highway funds, they had better pass laws lowering their state speed limits. If they don't, the feds will cut off the money. It's pure extortion. Medicare, Medicaid, unemployment, welfare, No Child Left Behind, and the state exchanges under Obamacare are just some examples. Want to get upstairs? Pay me. In this case it's more like, "Want me to pay you? Roll over."

The state assemblies, legislatures, and governors have to grow a backbone and tell the feds where to stick it. More important, they have to challenge the legal constitutional standing for the federal government to be passing these laws in the first place. If it isn't one of the eighteen powers we've covered, it is unconstitutional.

Tyranny isn't limited to the federal government. Unfortunately, the despotism runs rampant in our state capitals too. I live in New York. Half-jokingly, we call it either New Yorkistan or The People's Republic of New York. Granted, many unfunded mandates originate in Washington, trickle through the state capital, and hit our county and local governments, but not all of them. Using my own state as the example, in just education alone, New York has passed on more than one hundred unfunded mandates to the local school districts. Albany tells the school districts that they must carry out these additional functions but provide no funding. The school districts can't afford to do them and usually have to cut funding to other programs, such as art, music and theater.

According to the Citizen's Committee for an Effective Constitution (nyconstitution.org) in 2010, the unfunded mandates handed down by the state capital consumed $4 billion, or 90 percent, of all New York county property tax receipts. That's $4,000,000,000 that local communities in New York had to spend because the state government required their action but provided no funding.

The cost then trickles down from Washington, through the state capitols to our counties and towns. I asked a friend, Joe Lightfoot who is the Chair of the St. Lawrence County, NY Board of Legislators just what the impact of these mandates are on the county. I found his answer pretty shocking. He told me more than 90% of the county's tax levy goes straight to Albany to pay for unfunded mandates. 90%!!

He sent me the following figures from the county's budget:

"The following are the Nine (9) NYS mandates that wreak havoc with our budget.

| | 2014 | 2015 |
|---|---|---|
| Medicaid | 24.10 | 24.10 |
| Public Assistance | 2.60 | 2.80 |
| Child Welfare/Protective Services | 2.37 | 3.34 |
| Preschool/Special Education | 1.80 | 1.50 |
| Early Intervention | 0.40 | 0.40 |
| Probation | 2.80 | 2.70 |
| Indigent Defense | 2.20 | 2.10 |
| Youth Detention | 0.48 | 0.45 |
| Pension | 7.50 | 6.80 |
| total (in millions $$) | 44.25 | 44.19 |
| total tax levy (in millions $$) | 45.50 | 47.20 |

In FY 2014 the cost of these programs amounted to 97.25% of the total tax levy intake. You might also be aware that the County Jail is mandated by the State Department of Corrections to have a minimum number of staff and they set that number. That is an additional cost to the taxpayer. So much for home rule!!!" (6)

Often the county or town is forced to raise taxes to pay this bill. The citizens, of course, blame the county without realizing that it isn't really their fault. Just as the bill is punted down, blame should be passed all the way up to Washington.

Even if the state or federal government funded these programs, the money still comes from us. It's our money. If the local governments and school districts are to be forced to commit resources such as labor, clerical, time, and money to do something, I think they should have the power to decide whether they need to do it at all. Again, when power is retained closest to the citizen, it is most responsive, effective, and efficient.

Also, the closer we keep governance, the higher the value of the individual citizen. Most educational decisions, for example, should be between parents and teachers, with parents in charge. There will never be a one-size-fits-all program for teaching kids that will work. Every child is different. Now we have a federal Department of Education extorting the states to adopt the ridiculous and insidious Common Core, which promotes its cultural Marxist agenda. The states feel they have to take it or the feds will cut off their funding. They push this plus one hundred other mandates down to the local schools. All the while the First Lady sits in the White House deciding what your kids must have for lunch. In such a top-down omnipotent system, to our representatives in either Washington or your state capital, just what is the value of your child? Not much.

This isn't limited to just education. The same exact pattern is at work on every issue you can think of including housing, welfare, unemployment, and the environment. The list goes on and on. Your town board's hands are tied because the edict came from the county. Your county legislature's hands are tied because it came from the state. Your state's assembly's hands are tied because it came from Washington. No one ever seems to think—or better yet, stand up and scream—that the original law or regulation is illegal because Washington has no constitutional power over that issue in the first place. For crying out loud, enough is enough!

One hundred years ago, we gave a mouse a cookie. Now that mouse is our landlord.

# 9

# Turning the Tables

**"Three millions of people, armed with the holy cause of Liberty, and in such a country as that which we posses, are invincible by any force which our enemy can send against us."**

**—Patrick Henry**

The limitation of tyrants is the endurance of those they oppose.

—Frederick Douglas

We are fast approaching the stage of the ultimate inversion: the stage where the government is free to do anything it pleases, while the citizens may act only by permission; which is the stage of the darkest periods of human history, the stage of rule by brute force.

—Ayn Rand

That whenever any Form of Government becomes destructive of these ends, it is the Right of the People to alter or to abolish it, and to institute new Government, laying its foundation on such principles and organizing its powers in such form, as to them shall seem most likely to effect their Safety and Happiness.

—The Declaration of Independence

The times call for courage. The times call for hard work. But if the demands are high it is because the stakes are even higher. They are nothing less than the future of human liberty, which mean the future of civilization.

—Henry Hazlitt

What's the answer? The future looks bleak, but it doesn't have to be. We can still control its outcome. First, we have to acknowledge there is a problem. I think we can confidently say there is a problem. Second, we have to really believe we can effect change. You can. You are just as important as anyone else. What do Martin Luther King, Mother Theresa, Nelson Mandela, and George Washington all have in common? They're each only one person, the same as you. Get engaged. Take part. Don't sit this one out waiting for someone else to do it all for you. Be the change you want to see. Start right now acknowledging and really believing that you can change the world -because you can.

Too many of our people are openly defiant of the Creator and have neither the knowledge of nor the inclination to follow the laws of nature and nature's God. Our compliance with the oligarchy controlling our government and core institutions over time has destroyed the moral fiber of America, our family cohesion, and our sense of reliance on the providence of our Creator. We've allowed greed, envy, covetousness, pride, and arrogance to turn America into a curse in the world instead of the blessing our God intended. Maybe America can hold off the coming judgment through repentance and reconciliation; time will tell. This one thing is certain: if Americans refuse to fight and throw off the oligarchy and their agents, there will be an enormous cost in this land.

Inaction is surrender. Can you honestly claim to love your family while allowing them to face such a future? America's first struggle for liberty required the shedding of patriot blood. I sincerely hope and pray that it doesn't come to that this time. The price of freedom hasn't changed. It still takes courage, sweat and sacrifice. The wages of sin haven't changed either despite the wishes of people to the contrary.

Are you willing to pay the price for freedom, or will you allow the destruction of all you hold dear through inaction?

> You are the salt of the earth. But if the salt loses its saltiness, how can it be made salty again? It is no longer good for anything, except to be thrown out and trampled underfoot. You are the light of the world. A town built on a hill cannot be hidden. Neither do people light a lamp and put it under a bowl. Instead they put it on its stand, and it gives light to everyone in the house. In the same way, let your light shine before others, that they may see your good deeds and glorify your Father in heaven.
>
> —Jesus Christ, Matthew 5:13–16

Ours is the only country with a standard that sets God as our foundation, with the exception of Israel. There are about 250 million professing Christians of some flavor or denomination in America. People who claim to believe in the values of Christ are still a vast majority in our country. Any of the major groupings of American Christians—the 90 million evangelicals, 80 million

Catholics, or 80 million professing other Christians—could, if they voted together, elect the next president by themselves. It takes fewer than 70 million votes to elect a president.

Fifty-four million evangelicals decided not to vote in 2012. We could control the government for godly values, but instead of being the *light* of the world and the *salt* of the earth, we would rather sit and wait on Christ to come and rescue us. Have you considered that you were born right now, right where you are, because God has a job for you to do? Have you considered that God's calling, His special mission for your life, is to take part in the restoration of freedom and liberty? Just think of the implications of our success, not just for America but for the whole world!

So what if the world seems to be winning? We know the end of the story. But we also know what Christ said about being trampled upon when we lose our saltiness. That is why we are where we are today. We sat by and allowed Satan's agenda, done by a million little steps, get us to the point that in the freest country of the world, government can seriously persecute Christians. Too many of us relegated ourselves to the pews and did not go pull a lever. Then we go and pray as if He has not given us the power already.

Let us begin to lead the way, not just to salvation, but to peaceful government that allows free spreading of the gospel and all good things everywhere. If we do this thing willingly, we get a reward, but if we are unwilling, have we rejected the way, the truth, and the life?

> **Ephesians 6:11–18** Put on the whole armor of God that ye may be able to stand against the wiles of the devil.
>
> For we wrestle not against flesh and blood, but against principalities, against powers, against the rulers of the darkness of this world, against spiritual wickedness in high places.
>
> Wherefore take unto you the whole armor of God that ye may be able to withstand in the evil day, and having done all, to stand.

Before we launch out to change the world, we need to organize ourselves, plan, and prepare for what is ahead. We have to ask ourselves first, what is it we want to achieve? The sage advice from the great strategist Karl von Clauswitz is this: "No one starts a war—or rather, no one in his senses ought to do so—without first being clear in his mind what he intends to achieve by that war." (1) In simpler terms, we first identify what victory looks like. From there, we plan backward to now.

All of us have to examine our own lives. Are we living in accordance with Christ's teachings? If you are the husband and father in your household, are you the spiritual guide, teacher, and protector? Are you their leader, and are you being a leader worthy of the respect, trust, and faith of your family? If not, then you have some work to do before you can step out and lead others.

If you are the wife and mother in your household, do you live by Christ's teachings? Have you found a man worthy of following? Is he worthy of your trust, faith, respect, and love? Does he respect and love you as a partner while still being your leader and protector? If you are a single mother, are you a strong woman in God finding the strength to lead your children in God's grace? If not, you have some work to do before you can step out and lead others. And if you are a single mother, wait. Wait to find not just any man, but a godly man in every respect, one who is worthy of your trust and a proper godly guide for your kids.

Far be it from me to tell you how to live your lives, but let's face it. We're screwed. We really are. If we don't fix this country, we, our kids, and the world are doomed. I know this sounds extreme, but we really are doomed.

The war that we may have already lost wasn't fought with bombs and bullets; it was an insipidus war against our culture, our faith, God's law, and nature's law. To truly defeat it, we have to start there. We *have* to stand in defense of everything we know to be good, decent, and right. It is those principles that are being attacked. We must reinstate these core values in ourselves and within ourselves and our households first. As we've discussed, we simply cannot build strong communities, a strong town, and a strong country if our foundation is rotten. That foundation is first your faith. The next essential brick is the family.

Such a body of believers can do anything.

**Romans 8:31** What, then, shall we say in response to these things? If God is for us, who can be against us?

Be strong. We will certainly face slings and arrows, metaphorically speaking, so we cannot begin this struggle with faint hearts and unsure spirits. Find strength in our faith and find fellowship in other believers.

> Unborn ages and visions of glory crowd upon my soul, the realization of all which, however, is in the hands and good pleasure of Almighty God; but under his divine blessing, it will be dependent on the character and virtues of ourselves and of our posterity…if we and they shall live always in the fear of God, and shall respect his commandments…we may have the highest hopes of the future fortunes of our country…It will have no decline and fall. It will go on prospering…But if we and our posterity reject religious instruction and authority, violate the rules of eternal justice, trifle with the injunctions of morality, and recklessly destroy the political constitution which holds us together, no man can tell how sudden a catastrophe may overwhelm us that shall bury all our glory in profound obscurity. Should that catastrophe happen, let it have no history! Let the horrible narrative never be written!
>
> —Daniel Webster

So what do we do?

First, fear is the greatest weapon the enemy has to use against us. Do not be afraid. We are right. Stand up. Speak the truth in all things. Don't be cowed or silenced. They say sunlight is the best antiseptic; imagine what the light of Christ can do. Be the torch bearer. Others will rally to you. The natural tendency for most people is to sit and allow someone else to take that first step. Be the lion among sheep. If you find the strength within you to take that first step, your fearlessness will be contagious. Your one voice will become a chorus. Don't doubt yourself. You are not alone. The words of a wonderful song, *The Words I would Say*, by the Christian rock band Sidewalk Prophets come to mind:

> Be strong in the Lord and
> never give up hope.
> You're gonna do great things
> I already know
> God's got his hand on you so
> don't live life in fear
> forgive and forget
> but don't forget why you're here
> Take your time and pray
> Thank God for each day
> His love will find a way

In practical terms, the key is to get involved. Know what your kids are learning in school. Be engaged with their teachers and if you see something you don't agree with, speak up. Go public. I think you'll find that most other parents don't know what is going on and will be surprised when you tell them. Go to your school board meetings. Just go and listen. Watch and learn how issues are handled and what their priorities are. Then, become the fly in the ointment. If there is something amiss, don't allow it go unchallenged. Then start inviting your friends to come with you to the next meeting and then more to the next and so on. I know it will be hard to stand up in the middle of a meeting, all eyes on you and tell the emperor he has no clothes. That is why you need to find your strength within, with a strong family behind you and in our faith. When you are confident you are right, your heart and your faith will guide you. You and your voice count. Your opinion matters. There are probably others in the crowd who share your thoughts, but are waiting for someone else to say it out loud.

Make sure you are targeting the right people. When you speak before the board of education, make sure you are addressing issues they can change. Do the same with your county board of legislators, or a town hall meeting with an elected politician or candidate. That face to face interaction is critical. You have to go. Like the old saying goes, showing up is half the battle. It is so much easier to dismiss that comment on social media or an email. It is completely a different matter when they are standing face to face with a constituent or a disgruntled parent. When you go to these meetings, bring a friend. You'll find confidence with someone by your side.

Often you'll get the answer of "I'll get back with you on that" because you caught the board member or politician off guard. They're not really used to being cornered and questioned. If you do receive that answer, make sure you follow up. Call their office and press them for an answer. Don't let them off the hook just because they wanted to brush you off at the meeting. Then, make their answer public. Write a short letter to the editor on your exchange and what their final response was. You'll be surprised just how many people feel the exact same way as you do but never do anything about it.

Also, be there to back up others who are on our side. If someone else stands to make a comment or ask a question, let them know you're on their side. The board table isn't as intimidating when the citizen knows there are others who have their back in the crowd too. Then after the meeting get this person's contact information. Then, again, follow up. Call them or email them. Make plans to get together or go to the next meeting together. You've started to organize.

Another thing you should do is, as you are able, financially support organizations you believe in. You probably can't commit forty hours a week to activism but there are organizations who do have a full-time staff working on our behalf. By making even a small contribution to one of these groups, like the Patriot Institute, National Rifle Association, etc, you are having a greater impact than you may realize.

Expose others to your viewpoint. I recently watched a documentary about the prohibition movement. The 21st Amendment prohibiting the production, transport, and sale of alcohol was in effect, brought about by one man, Wayne Wheeler. Wayne believed in his cause, lobbied everyone and anyone he thought could help him achieve his objective, joined every anti-alcohol group he could find and rode his bicycle from town to town and door to door to sway public opinion in his favor. It worked. It worked so well that he was able to get an amendment to the US Constitution ratified. I don't expect any one person to be the next Wayne Wheeler, although that would be terrific, but together, we can have thousands of Wayne Wheelers working out there.

In your everyday, short letters to the editor, most of which today are posted online, can expose thousands of people in your community to your viewpoint. That can have a huge impact on public opinion. Use those opportunities to invite people to come out to the next school board, county board, city council or political town hall meeting. Watch as attendance grows. This will put those in power on notice that we are watching and will hold them accountable.

In regards to your children, you must be a teacher and mentor. Remember, kids today simply are not taught American history or civics in school anymore. Take every opportunity to gently instruct the kids in your life the truth about America. Be prepared to go slowly. Their indoctrination runs pretty deep, and they will defend their non-positions. These kids are taught what to think and what to feel; they aren't taught *how* to think. Generally speaking, our arguments depend on logic, reason, cause and effect, and even a little basic math. Today's generations don't learn how to logically support their positions. I engaged a liberal-minded person not too long ago on the topic of education funding. It was really hard to break through the person's sound argument of "I like it" using figures and logic. You'll invariably run into the same. We can't allow the voices of the schools, the media and Hollywood to be the only opinions our kids hear. The enemy can no longer control the narrative. You can always homeschool or send your kids to a good faith-based private school if you can afford it (and I know how expensive private schools can be).

All of this applies to your college-aged kids too. They'll believe whatever the collectivist cultural Marxists are telling them if those are the only ones talking. When choosing a college for your kids, be picky. College cost a huge amount of money. What is the product for which you're paying all that cash? What a racket the government and these schools have going! First, they convince everyone they need to go to college. Then, the government federalized the student loan program, so we have to borrow from the government. Then, when they get to school, we spend hundreds of thousands of dollars to pay for our kids to be indoctrinated into the collectivist mindset. Consider a Christian college instead. There are good choices out there. We're paying for it, shouldn't we be buying the product we want and not the one shoved down our throats?

When I think of the path ahead, I know the obstacles can seem insurmountable. When we have a recipe, a set of instructions to follow, it makes it easier. For instance, have you ever noticed just how many military terms are used in politics? Politicians devise their "strategy to win the "campaign." These terms are applicable because a political campaign can be planned in much the same way a military campaign. There is a strategy to meet objectives to take down an opponent in both scenarios. There is one planning tool in the military in particular we can apply to our movement to keep us focused and lead us to victory. I believe we can effectively use most of the nine principles of war, which are the following:

1. Mass—Concentrate combat power at the decisive place and time.
2. Objective—Direct every operation toward a clearly defined, decisive, and attainable goal.
3. Offensive—Seize, retain, and exploit the initiative.
4. Surprise—Strike the enemy at a time, at a place, or in a manner for which he is unprepared.
5. Economy of force—Allocate minimum essential combat power to secondary efforts.
6. Maneuver—Place the enemy in a position of disadvantage through the flexible application of combat power.
7. Unity of command—For every objective, ensure unity of effort under one responsible commander.

8. Security—Never permit the enemy to acquire an unexpected advantage.
9. Simplicity—Prepare clear, uncomplicated plans and clear, concise orders to ensure thorough understanding.

I won't spend a whole lot of time on these, but they apply. First, I want to be crystal clear on this: I am not in any way advocating violent actions of any kind. We can win this without firing a shot. We have to. Remember, the enemy thrives on chaos, so any of our actions that promote or bring on chaos work for the enemy. Nothing will more surely bring on the chaos in which the enemy thrives than our turning to any form of violence. We will win, and we will do it through God's love. We will do it by being the example of everything we want this world to be. We will win through peace.

Ok, back to the principles of war. Mass—Concentrate power at the decisive place and time. Have you noticed just how many groups have sprung up promoting this issue or that cause in the past few years? People, it seems, are starting to wake up. There are pro-gun and pro–Second Amendment groups, anti–Common Core groups, groups against illegal immigration, and a whole host of others. These also include the Tea Party and groups promoting the Constitution and our founding principles. Maybe you belong to one or more of these already. That's great, except for one thing. All of these efforts, however noble and worthwhile, dilute our political voice and strength.

We need to join together and unite for one common purpose. Instead of focusing on any one particular battle, we should concentrate on winning the war. Our enemy has had a one-hundred-year head start on us, and we have a lot of work to do. We can't afford to dissipate our collective power focusing on only one issue at a time. We are at war for the very survival of freedom on this earth. We have to — peaceably — start acting like it.

Together we can again be the shining city on a hill. We have to be the change we want to see. We have to be a light and set the example. Stand strong. Stand by our faith and our convictions. Others will follow. Too many are willing to let someone else carry the load and take all the risks. The time has passed for us to sit idly on the sidelines. With the full armor of God, we will prevail. When we win, our victory will turn all of these important and related issues around in our favor.

Second is this: Objective—Direct every operation toward a clearly defined, decisive, and attainable goal. If whatever we're doing doesn't directly contribute to victory, then we don't need to be doing it at all. Keep the goal in mind, and don't get distracted. We patriots need to keep our focus and drive to the end zone. This also keeps as many resources available as possible, including money, time, volunteers, and even flyers, letters to the editor, and so on to be directed toward our ultimate goal.

Offensive—Seize, retain, and exploit the initiative. The enemy has retained the initiative for far too long. Even those who were supposed to be the opposing party in Washington consistently roll over and immediately go on the defensive. That has to be over. We have to grow thick skins and be prepared to suffer the slings and arrows that the other side will throw at us. We are right. We know we are right. Let's take the offensive. Ride to the sound of the guns, metaphorically speaking, and let's take the fight to them. To paraphrase General Ulysses S. Grant, we need to stop worrying about what the bad guys might do to us and start making them worry about what we are doing to them.

Surprise—Strike the enemy at a time, at a place, or in a manner for which he is unprepared. Where is the enemy unprepared? I believe this starts from our pulpits. God and our faith are the foundation of our civilization and our liberty. Disconnecting us as a people from our faith is key to the enemy's success. Starting from our churches and our faith and working upward will grant us the element of surprise we need for our first and prolonged offensive. Everything else will emanate from there. This surprise "attack" will unbalance our adversary. Once they are unbalanced, we can seize and keep the initiative.

Economy of force—Allocate minimum essential combat power to secondary efforts. This is closely linked to mass. We can no longer allow the enemy to scatter us and our attention. Either we are working together on our objective, or we are allocating the minimum amount of resources toward other things that directly support our main objective. Everything else, important though it may be, will just have to wait.

Maneuver—Place the enemy in a position of disadvantage through the flexible application of combat power. We have to be faster, smarter, and more flexible than the enemy. If they think they can beat us on the Sunday talk shows, we create a peaceful incident that takes the wind out of their sails, and we then get our narrative on TV. If they can get a headline, we dominate the editorials and social media. If they think they can get their progressive mayor elected, then we flood the town with voter registrations and petitions, offer rides to the polls, and beat them. We have to work together! Let me say that again—*we have to work together*—and we can beat them at every turn and in every situation. They're weak. Their positions and their ideology are weak. They can only win through consistently lying and distorting the truth. The truth shall set us free, literally.

Unity of command—For every objective, ensure unity of effort under one responsible commander. This is the time for humility. It isn't important who is in charge. We have to humble ourselves before the Lord and His cause.

"If my people, who are called by my name, will humble themselves and pray and seek my face and turn from their wicked ways, then I will hear from heaven, and I will forgive their sin and will heal their land" (2 Chronicles 7–14).

Victory is the only thing that matters. All that is important is saving this country for our children and grandchildren. We all have to be equally prepared to lead and to follow. If one among us should fall, we all have to stand ready to pick up the lead and carry on. We all will be leaders. We all will be followers. When it is your time to lead, do so with all the humility that the cause deserves. When it is your time to follow, do so as if the fate of the entire endeavor hangs on your every action.

I founded the Patriot Institute to be that one place for all like-minded patriots to find groups in their respective areas and to communicate with leaders and organizers, and as a collection of reference materials to both educate and motivate us for the fight ahead. Our power increases exponentially when we join together. There are many, many terrific conservative groups out there. Imagine what we could accomplish if all the pro-life groups fighting against abortion, the 2nd Amendment groups fighting for our right to keep and bear arms, the anti-Common Core groups fighting for education and parental rights, Tea Party groups fighting for lower taxes and responsible government, and all the others came together as one! There would be nothing that could stand in our way. If you peel off the layers and look at the source, we are all fighting the same fight – individualism versus collectivism. Statism versus the rights and worth of the individual citizen. If we can fix that, we fix everything.

Security—Never permit the enemy to acquire an unexpected advantage. We have to be on our guard at all times. The enemy is the personification of deceit. The enemy will lie, send trolls to join our organization, and do everything and anything to disrupt our plans. Fabricated stories about our being racists, bigots, haters, and everything else you can think of will become their narrative. They will produce videos supposedly taken from inside our meetings or events that will be carefully edited to show what they want them to show. We have to not only root them out when we find them but also be ever vigilant to their schemes.

"The condition upon which God hath given liberty to man is eternal vigilance."

—John Philpot Curran

Let me say one more critical thing here. The best defenses against the enemy's lies, deceit, and schemes are love, honor, and honesty. Everything we do has to honor God. Our actions have to be undertaken as if they were our last act on this earth and the first thing we will answer for in our final judgment. We have to consistently be the polar opposite of the enemy we are confronting. Where they ferment violence, we embrace. Where they spur hatred, we have to spread love. When they lie, we shout the truth from the rooftops. Only then will our fight be righteous. That's how we win.

Finally, Simplicity—Prepare clear, uncomplicated plans and clear, concise orders to ensure thorough understanding. The best laid plans can get muddled up in execution. When we decide to act, our plans will be simple, truthful, and easy to execute. We will act as a team always and speak with one voice. Simple, easy-to-understand, and honest messages that are consistent throughout our organization will win the day.

Voting and elections. Are you registered to vote? If not, get registered. If your friends aren't registered to vote, get them registered as well. Voting is supposed be the individual's check on government power at every level. Use it. I would urge you to strongly consider not registering for one of the major parties. Register as an independent. See, if the parties really cared and found the best candidate not to just win the election but also do the best job of preserving liberty and defending the Constitution, and if they really, really got behind that candidate, they could win. As an independent, you can find, support, and then vote for the very best candidate for every office, from dog catcher to president. Why would you support a major party if it certainly doesn't support you?

You must also find and support great constitutional candidates at every level, from your local school board to the White House. If you know someone who would make a good candidate, talk to him or her about running. If you would make a good candidate, run. Support good candidates, too. Walk petitions, donate to their campaign, and really help to get their message out there. I know from experience that a good volunteer is worth his or her weight in gold to a campaign, especially an underdog or underfunded grassroots candidate. Then, of course, vote. Not only vote yourself, but also help others get to the polls. The other side is really good at getting out the vote. We, frankly, suck at it by comparison. We need to organize better and get this crucial part right.

But it will take more than just voting. The entire culture in our country has been perverted, diseased, and turned against us. The media, academia, and establishment of major political parties are all infiltrated. Clearly, fixing this is a much longer-term proposition, but it has to be done nonetheless.

When faced with what seemed an impossible task, we had a saying in the Army: "How do you eat an elephant? One bite at a time."

Remember, the Constitution is the supreme law of the land. Its basis is both common law and God's law. Just as no government can strip citizens of our natural, God-given rights, no government, judge, or other official appointed or elected to that government can legally infringe upon those rights. We the people shall remain the rightful masters of the government we created.

There have been several Supreme Court decisions that codify those notions in legal precedents:

> All laws, rules and practices which are repugnant to the Constitution are null and void.
>
> — *Marbury v. Madison*, 5th US (2 Cranch) 137, 180

> Where rights secured by the Constitution are involved, there can be no rule making or legislation which would abrogate them.
>
> — *Miranda v. Arizona*, 384 US 436, 491

Any legislation that violates God's law or the Constitution is automatically void. Where do you think our law comes from? Why isn't it ok for me to come to your house and shoot you in the head and take your property? Because to do so would be a violation of your basic God-given rights of life and property. If five people in the country, the required majority in Supreme Court cases, suddenly decide that it is ok for me to shoot you in the head and take your stuff, does that make it ok? No, it only makes it legal. Slavery was once legal in this country. So were Jim Crow laws, segregation and the rounding up and internment of Japanese Americans. Legal and right are often not at all the same thing.

The immediate steps that need to be taken to save this country are quite extensive and will seem daunting when viewed as a whole. Accomplishing the initiatives on this list may seem like an impossible pipe dream. We have to act and think like our enemies, only honestly, with honor, integrity, and responsibility. To them, even the smallest step toward accomplishing the ultimate goal is a victory. They never retreat, not one step, and only and always move forward. If they win a legislative victory in one state, they move to the next. If they lose in a referendum, they take their fight to the courts. If they lose in the courts, they take their fight to the streets.

We can't ever give up either. We can't ever think we can't do it or that we are too far gone. We must fight for, even struggle for, every little baby step if it is in the right direction. Then we have to hold onto that one inch of success and guard it. Then we take the next step. It will be a long struggle. In the end, we have to believe in our cause, and we have to win. One thing at a time. Together, we can accomplish anything.

This list encompasses the big, national initiatives that I feel are necessary to really make a significant difference in saving America, though it will not get done all at once.

1. Defund the United Nations. This international leftist organization has done nothing that supports the United States, our national heritage, or the liberty of our citizens. The UN has become nothing more than a cover group pushing for climate change and global redistribution of wealth, and is consistently just seeking more power at the expense of our national sovereignty. We need to stop paying for it.
2. Kick the United Nations out of our country. Lease the new available space for commercial use, a much better employment of that prime Manhattan real estate anyway.
3. Eliminate the US Department of Education. There is no provision whatsoever for education in the Constitution. The entire department is illegal and doesn't educate a single student. It is the national vehicle through which Common Core is being forced onto the states. Get rid of it.
4. Eliminate the Internal Revenue Service. Our vast and confusing tax code isn't being used to simply fund essential government functions.

Instead, our taxes are being used to promote political agendas to support or discourage behavior that our government deems we should or should not be engaged in. Get rid of it, and go to a flat tax based on percentage of income.

5. Eliminate other unconstitutional bureaucracies of the federal government starting with the following:
   a. Health and Human Services
   b. Housing and Urban Development (HUD)
   c. Department of Labor
   d. Department of Energy
   e. Environmental Protection Agency (EPA)
   f. Department of Agriculture

   With the elimination of these departments, all standing regulations connected to these departments automatically and immediately expire. Any and all functions formerly conducted by these useless bureaucracies can be done at the state level.
6. Through an Article V convention of states, propose the following amendments to the Constitution:
   a. Repeal the Seventeenth Amendment and give the states back the check on federal power that the founders intended.
   b. Repeal the Sixteenth Amendment to eliminate the IRS.
   c. Add an amendment to impose strict term limits on all members of the House of Representatives. Senators will be appointed by their state legislatures; they won't need term limits unless dictated by their respective state constitutions.
   d. Add a balanced budget amendment, with a provision exclusively for times of Congressionally-declared war and other national emergencies that would allow the federal government to borrow money as determined by Congress.
   e. Add an amendment that specifies there shall be no regulations or executive actions that would cost more than $100 million burden on our economy as a whole, and/or have penalties on individual citizens that would include the federal government

seizing personal property or could include prison terms. Anything meeting that criteria can only come from Congress as a law duly reviewed, voted on and passed by our elected representatives. This would eliminate any federal department, agency, or bureaucrat from writing regulations that result in citizens losing their property or being thrown in jail. Anything that could do that to an American citizen should have the force of law and face the review of our elected representatives.

f. Add an amendment that all laws proposed to Congress must have the exact article of the Constitution on it that gives the federal government jurisdiction to enact the law in the first place. If any proposed piece of legislation cannot be directly tied back to an enumerated power of the federal government in the Constitution, Congress will not be allowed to pass any legislation on it. Period.
g. Add an amendment that imposes a strict twelve-year term limit on members of the Supreme Court. Twelve years would ensure that members outlast any president who put them there, and they could vote their conscious in accordance with the Constitution. Additionally, members of SCOTUS can be recalled or impeached, as can any other federal official, in accordance with impeachment rules set forth in the Constitution. Article III, Section 1 of the Constitution states, "The Judges, both of the supreme and inferior Courts, shall hold their Offices during good Behaviour." If these judges are not acting in good behavior, as determined by Congress, they can be removed from the bench by Congress in accordance with the terms to be described in this amendment.
h. Add an amendment that all members of Congress are subject to the laws they pass. No exclusion or special privilege allowed.

The intent of all of these initiatives is to diffuse the power of the federal government. Any void left by eliminated agencies and departments will by necessity be taken up by the states. Or maybe it won't be, and that's ok too.

Some states may determine they don't need a state-run department of housing and urban development, for example. Fine. That is what the concept of state sovereignty is all about.

It is fortunate for us that the states can act on their own to add or repeal amendments to the Constitution. Our Framers wisely anticipated that we one day might have a federal government is simply out of control and is never going to correct itself. The Framers put a provision in the Constitution that allowed us to do just that, Article V:

> The Congress, whenever two thirds of both Houses shall deem it necessary, shall propose Amendments to this Constitution, or, on the Application of the Legislatures of two thirds of the several States, shall call a Convention for proposing Amendments, which, in either Case, shall be valid to all Intents and Purposes, as Part of this Constitution, when ratified by the Legislatures of three fourths of the several States, or by Conventions in three fourths thereof, as the one or the other Mode of Ratification may be proposed by the Congress; Provided that no Amendment which may be made prior to the Year One thousand eight hundred and eight shall in any Manner affect the first and fourth Clauses in the Ninth Section of the first Article; and that no State, without its Consent, shall be deprived of its equal Suffrage in the Senate.

The states, we the people, can change the Constitution. We are the ultimate check on federal power. I think the time has come for us to exercise that power. How?

There is a national convention of states project that is pushing and lobbying the state legislatures to sign on for an Article V convention of states to propose amendments to the Constitution. Look for the movement online. Contact them in your state and see what you can do to help.

The two established major parties, the Republicans and the Democrats, are a big part of the problem. When representatives of either party does something outrageous, instead of fixing the problem, the opposing party prefers to fix blame. For example, when the Democrats and the Obama Administration passed the Affordable Care Act, aka Obamacare, the Republicans screamed at the top of their lungs that they must regain control of Congress so they could repeal it. In a landslide election, they took the House of Representatives in 2010. Then, in 2012, American voters gave them control of the Senate. They have control of Congress. They haven't even so much as defunded Obamacare. According to the Constitution, the House has control of the money. Nothing happens in government until somebody writes a check. The Republican-controlled House continues to write the checks for not only Obamacare but every other policy, agency, program, and department that they complain about. Why?

Well, there is simply too much money in complaining about the other side. As a registered Republican, I have received hundreds of e-mail solicitations from the GOP that in effect said, "Look at what President Obama and the Democrats are up to now! Send us money!" Each side wants to use the evils of the other side to gain power in the next election. It's all a game to them.

I ran for Congress in 2010. As I made my way around to the various Republican county committees in my district, I was never once asked about my vision for America or my views on any topic whatsoever. All these party hacks wanted to know was how much money I had and how much money I could get. Winning was the only thing that mattered. I could have been Hitler incarnate; it didn't matter as long as I could put another "win" in the party scoreboard. That's at the county level. It gets much worse the higher in the chain you go. Also, there are party gatekeepers at every level in all parties. I remember being told that a state party leader said, "No one gets to Washington except through me." Sound familiar? "Want to get upstairs? Pay me."

The result of all these party politics is that by the time the citizens go into the voting booth, the choices they are presented with aren't necessarily the best candidates. They're not at all who even the party thinks will do the best job. No, the voter is presented with the candidates the parties believe have the best chances of winning. What they do, how they perform once they're in office, is of so little consequence to the parties that it is very rarely, if ever, spoken about before the election. All they want to do is win. These parties and our politicians keep shuffling the deck chairs on the *Titanic*, arguing over the color of the drapes as the ship sinks to the bottom. As long their party is the party that gets to finally pick the color of the drapes, all is good as far as they're concerned. That's a huge problem.

Jury nullification. Do you know what jury nullification is? This is a constitutionally protected power of we the people. We have a Fifth-Amendment right to a trial by a jury of our peers. It is not the primary function of the jury, as many think, to simply determine whether or not the defendant has committed (or not) the crime of which he or she is accused by government. No, its primary function is to first protect the jury's fellow citizen from tyrannical abuses of government.

The jury can decide that the law the citizen is accused of breaking is unjust and acquit that citizen. The jury can also decide that the punishment prescribed by the court is too severe and then either acquit or determine a different punishment more fitting to the crime. Even if it is beyond any doubt that the accused did actually commit the crime, the jury can, in effect, tell the court, "Yes he broke the law, but it is an unjust law," setting him free.

Here is the bottom line: we the people are the supreme rulers of government, even in the courtroom.

Not many people know of jury nullification. They should. A Supreme Court case, *Sparf v. United States*, upheld jury nullification in 1895. That ruling also included the provision that judges are not required to inform juries of nullification. So they don't. Part of our mission, then, is to do the following:

- Inform potential jurors of their traditional, legal authority to refuse to enforce unjust laws.
- Inform potential jurors that they cannot be required to check their consciences at the courthouse door.
- Inform potential jurors that they cannot be punished for their verdicts.
- Inform everyone that juror veto—jury nullification—is a peaceful way to protect human rights against corrupt politicians and government tyranny.

We have to remember, and inform other jurors and potential jurors, that the accused is not the only thing on trial. The law itself is on trial in every courtroom. If we ever find ourselves in the unfortunate position of being on trial ourselves, we have to inform the jury of their rights and of the power of jury nullification.

The great limit on jury nullification is that even when completely successful, it only applies to that one court case. Jury nullification does not overturn bad law. It may save one citizen from being the victim of bad law or excessive punishment, but that's all. It only applies to that one defendant in that one case. It would probably take a massive number of cases to be thrown out through jury nullification to have any lasting impact on the law in any state or across the country.

As we discuss jury nullification, I'd like to use this as an opportunity to show how our faith can sustain us in this struggle. On November 24th, 2015, former Christian pastor, Keith Wood was handing out pamphlets on jury nullification in front of the courthouse in Grand Rapids, Michigan. "I'm a disciple of Jesus Christ," said Wood, who explained his decision to hand out the fliers he received from a Montana-based organization. "Jesus said 'the truth will set you free' and I want people to know the truth." (2)

When that day's presiding judge got wind of what was going on in front of his court, he had Wood arrested. Mecosta County District Court Judge Peter Jaklevic charged Wood with jury tampering, a misdemeanor and obstruction of justice, a felony. Wood could face up to five years in prison. Keith Wood stuck to his guns because he was absolutely within his rights to inform others of their rights. "If you don't use your rights, you lose them," Wood said. (3) At this writing, the case has yet to be settled, but Judge Jaklevic has recused himself from the case.

The point is, as you move forward, you can expect opposition from those who today hold the power. We have to be strong enough, and be in the right, to stand our ground and not back down, not only as Keith Wood has, but as so many others who fought with peace and righteousness.

As I write this, we are fourteen months away from the 2016 presidential election. There is a whole new generation of Americans—at least I hope they are Americans—who will be participating in their very first presidential election. At eighteen years old, the new crop of voters was born in 1998. The only president in their living memory is Barack Obama, who took office when they were ten years old. These new voters have no idea what conservatism is. They have no concept of an America without Obamacare, open borders, Common Core, open homosexuality in our military, or an America with a thriving economy. They have nothing in their lives to use as a comparison with today's America. Think of that for a moment. Ever explain algebra to a hamster? Talking to them about what freedom is and trying to explain what America should be will be much the same situation as one in which I found myself in Baghdad. Freedom is a hard concept to understand if you've never experienced it before. This mission is made all the harder because while we're talking to them, they are bombarded every day, from every direction, with the cultural Marxist message. Again, baby steps. Those steps must start in your living room or in your car. Wherever you find yourself in a position to spread our message, especially to the younger generations, take advantage of it.

There have been so many scandals in Washington since President Obama took office. A short list of these scandals and governmental embarrassments isn't short.

The most insidious among the many includes Operation Fast and Furious, where thousands of assault weapons were released to the Mexican drug cartels. Border Patrol Agent Brian Terry and hundreds of Mexicans have been killed by these weapons, and the White House and the Justice Department covered it up.

In addition, the IRS was caught illegally targeting conservative and religious groups that the White House believed would oppose Obama's reelection.

Then there's unconstitutional Obamacare, the Benghazi cover-up, weapon sales to Islamic rebel groups in Syria and Libya, the Veteran Administration allowing our veterans to die while waiting on secret lists for care that was never coming, and on and on.

But even these are not the biggest scandal of all. No, the biggest scandal of all is that really, nobody cares.

A recent Gallop poll asked one thousand Americans, "Are you satisfied or dissatisfied with your freedom to choose what to do with your life?" Only 21 percent of respondents said they were dissatisfied. So 79 percent are satisfied with the lack of freedom to choose what to do with their lives. That's scary.

Most Americans don't question why they are being felt up at the airport or why the NSA (if they even know what the NSA is) is listening to their phone calls, or why the first lady in Washington is dictating what their kids eat at school. Just in 2015 alone, the Supreme Court has decided it has the power to legislate from the bench and shred the First, Fourth, Ninth, and Tenth Amendments.

The justices have ruled that police do not need a warrant to ransack your home if you're not there. The court also ruled the police may enter and turn your home upside down if any person in the house consents. (4) The Supreme Court has ruled that same-sex marriage is legal in all fifty states despite the fact that "marriage" appears nowhere in the Constitution and is not a power of the federal government. But really, none of that matters.

By and large, the American public does not think beyond the issue of the moment. The media proclaims the same-sex marriage issue is only about equality, without regard to the constitutional precedent, and the average apathetic American cheers.

It isn't all their fault. They are taught in schools to "feel" and not to think. They feel global warming is real. They can't produce any supporting facts. They are taught to "feel" sorry for the poor and underprivileged third-world kids illegally coming across the border. They aren't taught the economics of providing a huge welfare state and open borders and how that will bankrupt any nation.

They are taught to "feel" angry at the rich because somehow they have stolen their money from the poor who would otherwise be rich. Today's students are taught to "feel" there are classes of people that are, or should be, protected and are somehow more "equal" than the rest of us. A gay couple can sue a Christian-owned bakery and have the government force the business to bake a cake for a gay marriage even though the ceremony is contrary to the bakery owners' religious beliefs. It is politically correct to stand up for the gay couple but certainly not for the Christians.

Today's students are, overall, ignorant of American history and basic civics. They are fed the lines and lies of nihilism versus government control. If you don't want Obamacare, then you must want people to die without health care. If you don't believe in global warming, or "climate change," then you hate polar bears. If you are against open borders, then you are selfish and want to deny undocumented workers the American dream, the same dream your immigrant ancestors had. If you fear that the same-sex ruling grants the federal government extra-constitutional powers and will ultimately destroy the institution of the family, you're a homophobe and a bigot.

The Constitution is no longer taught in schools, so more and more Americans are unable to identify when the government acts unconstitutionally. American students now don't know who won the Civil War or why it was fought. They don't know why or when the American Revolution took place. With no sense of history, there is no pride in being American.

Recently, after relating how "America" invaded Hawaii and took its queen prisoner, a fifteen-year-old high school freshman girl commented, "I hate Americans." That statement about sums up the leftist, progressive, Common Core–pushing education system at work in our schools.

It is the Left's intent to destroy every institution that lies between the individual and the state. Abortion and the welfare state destroy families. The courts will drive God and Christianity out of the schools and the public square. A completely biased media will feed the people still watching the state's propaganda. Schools will preach the Left's agenda as science and will dumb down our kids until they no longer possess or use any critical-thinking skills. After all of that, control is easy.

So why hasn't anyone gone to prison for all of the recent scandals? How can the government get away with shredding the Constitution and our rights? Easy; teach the people to watch *The Walking Dead* and *The Real Housewives*, and they'll never notice.

Power, as in political power, is used to bend others' will. No one who seeks it to take away the liberty of others can legitimately claim to love their neighbors.

Liberty, on the other hand, is consistent both with self-love and love of others because we must be willing to grant liberty to others to have it for ourselves. When people are ready, change will happen. Right now, most people want liberty for themselves but not for their neighbors. Obviously, that won't work. We must be caring enough to allow others to be free if we want freedom for ourselves.

Cultural Marxists have been working overtime for well over one hundred years to take down their "ripest apple on the tree," the United States. They have spent so much time and energy on America because we represent everything they despise. They also know that if they could just get America out of the way, with our deep-rooted values, shared history, and heritage—and especially, our faith and belief in God—then the whole world must follow.

I fear that unless God-fearing patriots who love this wonderful country don't stand together now and take action, America may fall into the dustbin of history.

The enemy's attack started with taking over our media, entertainment, and especially our schools to then slowly but surely indoctrinate each successive generation to adopt his ways. It has worked and is still working. Our families are dysfunctional, unborn babies are a "choice" to exterminate, and our churches are empty. More and more Americans fall into poverty and become enslaved to the state through the government's legal plunder and redistribution. Government assumes more and more control over every aspect of our lives, and most of our fellow citizens barely notice.

I believe the enemy can still be beaten. It won't be easy, and it won't be overnight. It will take unity, organization, and every ounce of our unwavering faith in the Almighty. With the full armor of God, standing shoulder to shoulder, we can win. We must win. The fate of future generations depends on what we do right now. Dr. Joseph Warren, president of the Massachusetts Congress before the American Revolution, said this to his fellow Americans:

> Our country is in danger, but not to be despaired of...On you depend the fortunes of America. You are to decide the important questions upon which rests the happiness and the liberty of millions yet unborn. Act worthy of yourselves.

What is America worth? What would you be willing to sacrifice to guarantee liberty for your children and their children? I believe, from the depths of my soul, that this country, this land of liberty, is worthy of "our best effort, and our willingness to believe in ourselves and to believe in our capacity to perform great deeds," as Ronald Reagan so eloquently stated in his first inaugural address. In his words, we must "believe that together, with God's help, we can and will resolve the problems which now confront us." (5)

As you take up this noble struggle, know with certainty that you are not alone. There are millions and millions of Americans who feel as you do. They, like you, see what is going on and know something must be done. Its starts with you. Its starts with all of us freedom-loving patriots who finally decide to act with compassion, love, honor, and God's grace.

Together we will prevail.

Think, just think of the America we are going to create! Every citizen will again feel free and raise their children in liberty. Our schools will once again teach basic math, along with critical-thinking and problem-solving skills. Our children will once again grow up knowing the true history and civics of the greatest country on earth. The entire relationship between we the people and the government we created to serve us will once again be restored to its proper place. Private property rights will be respected and businesses allowed to thrive and flourish without the choking yoke of unconstitutional regulations, rules, and fees strangling American prosperity.

Most important, when we win, the basic value of each and every citizen as guaranteed by the Bill of Rights and God's law will be restored and enshrined in our national framework.

We must keep our faith. We have to believe in ourselves and in the power of the Lord.

> **Matthew 14:22–33** Immediately, Jesus made the disciples get into the boat and go on ahead of him to the other side, while he dismissed the crowd. After he had dismissed them, he went up on a mountainside by himself to pray. Later that night, he was there alone, and the

> boat was already a considerable distance from land, buffeted by the waves because the wind was against it.
>
> Shortly before dawn Jesus went out to them, walking on the lake. When the disciples saw him walking on the lake, they were terrified. "It's a ghost," they said, and cried out in fear.
>
> But Jesus immediately said to them: "Take courage! It is I. Don't be afraid."
>
> "Lord, if it's you," Peter replied, "tell me to come to you on the water."
>
> "Come," he said.
>
> Then Peter got down out of the boat, walked on the water, and came toward Jesus. But when he saw the wind, he was afraid and, beginning to sink, cried out, "Lord, save me!"
>
> Immediately Jesus reached out his hand and caught him. "You of little faith," he said, "why did you doubt?"

I know we can do it. When our boat is rocking on stormy seas, it isn't time to give up. Have faith! We are being called upon to pull ourselves up from the bottom, step off the rocky deck and out onto the water. I know that together, with God's help, we can do anything. Now is our moment. Now, right now, is the time for us to stand together and honorable, peaceably, and righteously take this great country back!

# Sources Cited and References

## Cover Photograph: Daisy Hecker

### Introduction

1. Thelen Paulk, "A Visitor from the Past" Copyright 1986, http://www.angelfire.com/mo/greendragon1/page39.html
2. Ronald Reagan "A Time for Choosing" speech in support of presidential candidate Barry Goldwater, October 27, 1964, http://www.reagan.utexas.edu/archives/reference/timechoosing.html

### Chapter 1

1. Samuel Adams, one of the most ardent of the Founding Fathers in his desire for independence from England, delivered this speech to a large audience at the State House in Philadelphia on August 1, 1776. Adams, a signer of the Declaration of Independence, also served as Delegate to the First Continental Congress in 1774 and was elected Governor of Massachusetts in 1794. http://www.nationalcenter.org/SamuelAdams1776.html
2. Michael Minnicino, The New Dark Age, The Frankfurt School and Political Correctness, Winter, 1992 *issue of FIDELIO Magazine*, http://www.schillerinstitute.org/fid_91-96/921_frankfurt.html
3. Ibid

4. Ibid
5. *Walter Benjamin, The Arcades Project*, trans. Howard Eiland & Kevin McLaughlin, Cambridge, MA. & London: Belknap Press, 1999.
6. Max Horkheimer and Theodor W. Adorno, Dialectic of Enlightenment: Philosophical Fragmentsis translated from Volume 5 of Max Horkheimer, Gesammelte Schriften: Dialektik der Aufklärung und Schriften 1940–1950, edited by Gunzelin Schmid Noerr, ©1987 by S. Fishcher Verlag GmbH, Frankfurt am Main. Stanford University Press, Stanford, CA 2002
7. Robin Phillips, The Illusionist How Herbert Marcuse Convinced a Generation that Censorship Is Tolerance & Other Politically Correct Tricks http://www.salvomag.com/new/articles/salvo20/herbert-marcuse-censorship-is-tolerance.php#sthash.FNFLwGfo.dpuf

**Chapter 2**

1. From the diaries of William Bradford, first Governor of the Plymouth settlement, quoted in The Pilgrims' Failed Experiment with Socialism, 2013, http://www.tpnn.com/2013/11/27/the-pilgrims-failed-experiment-with-socialism-2/
2. Ibid
3. Ibid
4. Wall Street Journal online, Venezuela's Food Shortages Trigger Long Lines, Hunger and Looting, Violent clashes flare in pockets of the country as citizens wait for hours for basics, such as milk and rice, by Maolis Castro and Kejal Vyas, Aug. 26, 2015 5:30 a.m. ET, http://www.wsj.com/articles/venezuelas-food-shortages-trigger-long-lines-hunger-and-looting-1440581400
5. Miton Freidman made these comments during an interview on the Phil Donahue show where he absolutely schooled Phil on the benefits free market capitalism and private property rights, 1979, https://www.youtube.com/watch?v=IYNSrQLtjKI

6. Maximilien François Marie Isidore de Robespierre (6 May 1758 – 28 July 1794) was one of the leaders of the French Revolution. Also known as "the Incorruptible". He was an influential member of the Committee of Public Safety and was instrumental in the period of the Revolution commonly known as the Reign of Terror that ended with his arrest and beheading by guillotine. Original French: *Le secret de la liberté est d'éclairer les hommes, comme celui de la tyrannie et de les retenir dans l'ignorance* Oeuvres, Volume 2 p. 253, first published in 1794. *Speeches of Maximilien Robespierre* (New York : International Publishers, 1927). Library of Congress Call Number DC146 .R6 A47; this is the only English language collection of Robespierre's speeches that is available
7. Michael Martinez and Jaqueline Hurtado, "Undocumented immigrants picked for city posts say U.S. is 'progressing'," 8 August 2015, CNN Online, http://www.cnn.com/2015/08/08/us/huntington-park-undocumented-immigrants-city-commission-appointees/
8. Steven Ertelt "Hundreds of thousands gather for record-breaking March for Life," 25 January 2013, LifeNews.com, http://www.lifenews.com/2013/01/25/hundreds-of-thousands-gather-for-record-breaking-march-for-life/
9. 2015 University of Missouri protests, https://en.wikipedia.org/wiki/2015_University_of_Missouri_protests Finding the actual number of students who took part in the protests proved to be problematic. There were many, many, many stories on the protests, but hardly any at all that stated a definitive number of participants. To the progressive media, it wasn't the scope of the incident, but its political motivation that really mattered.
10. Arlette Saenz, "President Obama praises University of Missouri protesters: "I want an activist citizenry," 15 November 2015, ABC News online, http://abcnews.go.com/Politics/president-obama-praises-university-missouri-protesters-activist-citizenry/story?id=35203826

11. Robert Tracinski, "Seven big failed environmentalist predictions" The Federalist online, 24 April 2015, http://thefederalist.com/2015/04/24/seven-big-failed-environmentalist- predictions/
12. Michael Minnicino, The New Dark Age, The Frankfurt School and Political Correctness, Winter, 1992 *issue of FIDELIO Magazine*, http://www.schillerinstitute.org/fid_91-96/921_frankfurt.html
13. Common Core forcing Marxism/Nazism on America's children, Sher Zieve, May 9, 2013 http://www.renewamerica.com/columns/zieve/130509
14. Personal Liberty, "High school students asked to answer questions about parents' gun ownership," by Sam Rolley, 28 September, 2015, http://personalliberty.com/high-school-students-asked-to-answer-questions-about-parents-gun-ownership/ see also World Net Daily, "High school questionnaire: Do your parents own guns?" Cheryl Chumley, 30 September, 2015, http://www.wnd.com/2015/09/high-school-questionnaire-do-your-parents-own-guns/ Also, America's Freedom Fighters, "URGENT: Texas High School is asking students these 10 outrageous questions, parents are furious", Dean James, 28 September, 2015, http://www.americasfreedomfighters.com/2015/09/28/urgent-texas-high-school-is-asking-students-these-10-outrageous-questions-parents-are-furious/#
15. Common Core forcing Marxism/Nazism on America's children, Sher Zieve, May 9, 2013 http://www.renewamerica.com/columns/zieve/130509
16. Ibid
17. President Barack Obama in an interview with the *San Francisco Chronicle*, January 17, *2008* https://www.youtube.com/watch?v=DpTIhyMaNw
18. Michael Minnicino, The New Dark Age, The Frankfurt School and Political Correctness, Winter, 1992 *issue of FIDELIO Magazine*, http://www.schillerinstitute.org/fid_91-96/921_frankfurt.html
19. Marcus Tullius Cicero *On Duties (De Officiis)*, Book I, Chapter 4, was written in October–November 44 BC

20. Edmund Burke, *A Vindication of Natural Society: or, a View of the Miseries and Evils arising to Mankind from every Species of Artifical Society. In a Letter to Lord ** by a Late Noble Writer,* ed. Frank N. Pagano (Indianapolis: Liberty Fund, Inc., 1982).
21. Michael Snyder, 40 Signs That We Have Seriously Messed Up The Next Generation Of Americans, Investment Watch Blog, 2 September 2012, http://investmentwatchblog.com/40-signs-that-we-have-seriously-messed-up-the-next-generation-of-americans/
22. Lyndon B. Johnson to two governors aboard Air Force One, 1964 as quoted by Ronald Kessler, *Inside the White House*, Pocket Books, 1995, ISBN: 0-671-87919-7. Apparently the quote was overheard by a Secret Service agent. Lyndon Johnson was known for his racism, including a taped phone conversation where he uses the "N" word: "but I have to prove it discriminates. I can't prove it in Texas. There's more niggers voting there than white folks." https://www.youtube.com/watch?v=r1rIDmDWSms

    I contacted the author, Ronald Kessler and was told "A champion of African-Americans, Johnson marshaled support from southern Democrats for his civil rights legislation. But his hypocrisy extended to regularly referring to blacks as "niggers." On Air Force One, Johnson was discussing his proposed civil rights bill with two governors. Explaining why it was so important to him, MacMillan [Air Force One steward Robert M. MacMillan] remembers that Johnson said it was simple: "I'll have them niggers voting Democratic for two hundred years." Email to author from Ronald Kessler 24 October 2015.
23. Joel Landau and Ginger Adams Otis, "Kentucky Clerk Kim Davis is free after 5 days in jail would not say if she would abide by judge and not interfere with issuing gay marriage licenses" 1 October 2015, New York Daily News online http://www.nydailynews.com/news/crime/kim-davis-freer-americans-lawyer-article-1.2352035
24. Stephen Dinan, "Number of sanctuary cities grows to 340; thousands of illegals released to commit new crimes" 8 October 2015, The Washington

Times online http://www.washingtontimes.com/news/2015/oct/8/number-of-sanctuary-cities-grows-to-340-thousands-/?page=all

As this article describes, and although I didn't bring it up in the text, the Obama administration is systematically releasing convicted illegal alien criminals from prison. Even the felons among these people do not face deportation, another example of the Left's successful program in indoctrination where the "foot soldier" of the progressive liberal will not discern right from wrong, good from evil, legal from illegal as they are being played by the establishment as they strive to change the demographics of the country to favor their party. That is a discussion worthy of several books in itself.

25. Pastor Chuck Baldwin, An Open Letter to My Fellow Pastors and Christians, website Chuck Baldwin Live, Published: Thursday, July 16, 2015, http://chuckbaldwinlive.com/Articles/tabid/109/ID/3340/An-Open-Letter-To-My-Fellow-Pastors-And-Christians.aspx
26. "Student reportedly suspended after saying "Bless you," NBC WMC Action News online, 20 August 2014, http://www.wmcactionnews5.com/story/26320134/dyer-county-student-reportedly-suspended-after-saying-bless-you
27. Todd Starnes, "Teacher tells student he can't read the Bible in classroom," Todd's American Dispatch, Fox News Opinion online, 5 May 2014, http://www.foxnews.com/opinion/2014/05/05/teacher-tells-student-cant-read-bible-in-my-classroom.html
28. Eric Rich, "Bible-reading student gets lesson in litigation" 3 October 2006, The Washington Post online, http://www.washingtonpost.com/wp-dyn/content/article/2006/10/02/AR2006100201238.html
29. The News Nerd Staff, "Boy suspended from school for reading the Bible during recess," 1 July 2015, The News Nerd, http://www.thenewsnerd.com/local/boy-suspended-school-reading-bible-recess/
30. Thomas Jefferson in a letter to the Danbury Baptist Association of Connecticut, 1 January 1802, Library of Congress Information Bulletin, June 1998, http://www.loc.gov/loc/lcib/9806/danpre.html. The complete letter reads:

To messers. Nehemiah Dodge, Ephraim Robbins, & Stephen S. Nelson, a committee of the Danbury Baptist association in the state of Connecticut.

Gentlemen

The affectionate sentiments of esteem and approbation which you are so good as to express towards me, on behalf of the Danbury Baptist association, give me the highest satisfaction. My duties dictate a faithful and zealous pursuit of the interests of my constituents, and in proportion as they are persuaded of my fidelity to those duties, the discharge of them becomes more and more pleasing.

Believing with you that religion is a matter which lies solely between Man and his God, that he owes account to none other for his faith or his worship, that the legitimate powers of government reach actions only, and not opinions, I contemplate with sovereign reverence that act of the whole American people which declared that their legislature should "make no law respecting an establishment of religion, or prohibiting the free exercise thereof," thus building a wall of separation between Church and State. Adhering to this expression of the supreme will of the nation in behalf of the rights of conscience, I shall see with sincere satisfaction the progress of those sentiments which tend to restore to man all his natural rights, convinced he has no natural right in opposition to his social duties.

I reciprocate your kind prayers for the protection and blessing of the common father and creator of man, and tender you for yourselves and your religious association, assurances of my high respect and esteem.

Th Jefferson

Jan. 1, 1802.

31. Matthew West, "Do Something" Copyright 2014 Sparrow Records

## Chapter 3

1. Nikolai Bukharin and Evgenii Preobrazhensky, "The ABC of Communism", Part Two: Practical - The Dictatorship of the Proletariat and the Upbuilding of Communism, XI. Communism and Religion, 1920, Penguin Books, 1969, First Published in English: 1922, Online Version: Marxists Internet Archive (marxists.org) 2001, Transcription/Markup: Mathias Bismo, https://www.marxists.org/archive/bukharin/works/1920/abc/11.htm
2. Benjamin Rush, "Of the mode of education proper in a republic" 1798, Selected Writings 87--89, 92, 94—96, http://press-pubs.uchicago.edu/founders/documents/v1ch18s30.html Benjamin Rush was an amazing man and arguably the most influential of our Founding Fathers. He was a physician, (and known as the "Father of American Medicine"), educator (and known as the "Father of Public Schools"), public official, philanthropist, member of the Continental Congress, signer of The Declaration of Independence, Treasurer of the U.S. Mint under Presidents Adams, Jefferson, and Madison, founder of the Pennsylvania Society for Promoting the Abolition of Slavery, member of the Abolition Society, and founder and president of the Philadelphia Bible Society. http://ringthebellsoffreedom.com/Quotes/brushcontent.htm
3. President Obama news conference 22 July 2009. He twisted his statement about the Gates arrest into a broader statement on racism at the end with "what I think we know separate and apart from this incident is that there's a long history in this country of African-Americans and Latinos being stopped by law enforcement disproportionately. That's just a fact."
4. President Obama news conference July 19, 2013.
5. Barack Obama, *Dreams of my Father,* 1995 Times Books, an imprint of Crown Books, a division of Random House. ISBN 1-4000-8277-3.
6. Frédéric Bastiat, page 2, *The Law,* first published in 1850, Copyright 2007 by the Ludwig von Mises Institute, Auburn, Alabama, ISBN:

978-1-933550-14-5; *The Law*, first published as a pamphlet in June, 1850, is already more than a hundred years old. And because its truths are eternal, it will still be read when another century has passed. Frederic Bastiat (1801-1850) was a French economist, statesman, and author. He did most of his writing during the years just before — and immediately following — the Revolution of February 1848. This was the period when France was rapidly turning to complete socialism. As a Deputy to the Legislative Assembly, Mr. Bastiat was studying and explaining each socialist fallacy as it appeared. And he explained how socialism must inevitably degenerate into communism. But most of his countrymen chose to ignore his logic. *The Law* is here presented again because the same situation exists in America today as in the France of 1848. The same socialist-communist ideas and plans that were then adopted in France are now sweeping America. The explanations and arguments then advanced against socialism by Mr. Bastiat are — word for word — equally valid today. His ideas deserve a serious hearing. http://bastiat.org/en/the_law.html

7. John Adams, Letter to the Officers of the First Brigade of the Third Division of the Militia of Massachusetts, 11 October 1798*, The Works of John Adams* (Boston, 1854), vol. 9, pp. 228-9.
8. The Harold and Presbyter, July 5th 1922, First Presbyterian Church, Macomb Illinois, Reverend William T. Rogers, D.D., Pastor.
9. Paul Harvey, "If I were the devil," 3 April 1965, text printed online, "Paul Harvey's warning to America: If I were the devil," 23 March 2012, The Truth Wins website, http://thetruthwins.com/archives/paul-harveys-warning-to-america-if-i-were-the-devil
10. Michael Minnicino, The New Dark Age, The Frankfurt School and Political Correctness, Winter, 1992 *issue of FIDELIO Magazine*, http://www.schillerinstitute.org/fid_91-96/921_frankfurt.html
11. Saul D. Alinsky, *Rules for Radicals, A practical primer for realistic radicals,* Acknowledgements, p.5, Copyright 1971 by Saul Alinsky, Random House.

## Chapter 4

1. Unnatural Deaths in the U.S.S.R.: 1928-1954 Paperback – January 1, 1983 by Iosif G. Dyadkin (Author), Nicholas Eberstadt (Introduction)
2. Che Guevara, "Tactics and Strategies of the Cuban Revolution", Revista Verde Olivo, Prensa Latina 8-10-68.
3. Daniel J. Goldhagen, *Hitler's Willing Executioners*, 1996, p. 20. In his work, Goldhagen makes the case that the Holocaust was genocide on an industrial scale. When interviewing those citizens who actually pulled the triggers or filled the gas chambers - the SS soldiers, the Gestapo police officers and the like - to examine their state of mind at the time, Goldhagen found a universal lack of empathy for their victims. The complete quotes from the perpetrators are: "It did not at all occur to me that these orders could be unjust. I was then of the conviction that the Jews were not innocent but guilty. I believed the propaganda that all Jews were criminals and subhumans and that they were the cause of Germany's decline after the First World War. The thought that one should disobey or evade the order to participate in the extermination of the Jews did not therefore enter my mind at all." As yet another genocidal executioner, speaking for all his brethren, states, "The Jew was not acknowledged by us to be a human being." So effective was the propaganda that these government employees murdered over 6 million men, women and children because the government told them to do it.
4. Margaret Sagner, Commenting on the 'Negro Project' in a letter to Dr. Clarence Gamble, December 10, 1939. - Sanger manuscripts, Sophia Smith Collection, Smith College, Northampton, Massachusetts. Also described in Linda Gordon's *Woman's Body, Woman's Right: A Social History of Birth Control in America*. New York: Grossman Publishers
5. William F. Jasper, "Obama's friend Ayers: Kill 25 million Americans," The New American, 31 October 2008, http://www.thenewamerican.com/usnews/politics/item/2455-obamas-friend-ayers-kill-25-million-americans The interview of Larry Grathwohl was part of an

anti-terrorism documentary, *No Place to Hide: The Strategy and Tactics of Terrorism* by the Western Goals Foundation in 1982. An excerpt of the Grathwohol interview titled "Larry Grathwohl interview about William Ayers, Obama's Mentor" can be seen here: https://www.youtube.com/watch?v=VlN2t0oERHk and a longer 36 minute short documentary on the Weather Underground, "Bringing Down America by Larry Grathwohl" here: https://www.youtube.com/watch?v=b9iwcyjmgZg

In 1974 Ayers co-authored, along with his wife Bernadine Dohrn, Jeff Jones, and Celia Sojourn, a book titled *Prairie Fire: The Politics of Revolutionary Anti-Imperialism.* This book contained the following statements:

- "We are a guerrilla organization. We are communist women and men ... deeply affected by the historic events of our time in the struggle against U.S. imperialism."
- "Our intention is to disrupt the empire, to incapacitate it, to put pressure on the cracks, to make it hard to carry out its bloody functioning against the people of the world, to join the world struggle, to attack from the inside."
- "The only path to the final defeat of imperialism and the building of socialism is revolutionary war."
- "Revolutionary war will be complicated and protracted. It includes mass struggle and clandestine struggle, peaceful and violent, political and economic, cultural and military, where all forms are developed in harmony with the armed struggle."
- "Without mass struggle there can be no revolution.
  Without armed struggle there can be no victory."
- "We need a revolutionary communist party in order to lead the struggle, give coherence and direction to the fight, seize power and build the new society."
- "Our job is to tap the discontent seething in many sectors of the population, to find allies everywhere people are hungry or angry, to mobilize poor and working people against imperialism."

- "Socialism is the total opposite of capitalism/imperialism. It is the rejection of empire and white supremacy. Socialism is the violent overthrow of the bourgeoisie, the establishment of the dictatorship of the proletariat, and the eradication of the social system based on profit."

**Chapter 5**

1. Edmund Burke, *"A Vindication of Natural Society: or, a View of the Miseries and Evils arising to Mankind from every Species of Artifical Society," In a Letter to Lord ** by a Late Noble Writer,* first published anonymously in 1756, *ed. Frank N. Pagano (Indianapolis: Liberty Fund, Inc., 1982). 12/20/2015. http://oll.libertyfund.org/titles/850*
2. Marcus Tullius *Cicero, Cicero De Officiis (On Duties), Book I, Chapter 4, 44 B.C.*
3. Benjamin Franklin, Advice to a Young Man on the Choice of a Mistress, June 25, 1745

**Chapter 6**

1. Mike Church, from The Mike Church Radio Show and transcript article, "What Is The Greatest Phrase Ever?" June 26, 2015, http://www.mikechurch.com/transcripts/what-is-the-greatest-phrase-ever/
2. Ibid
3. Frederic Bastiat, *The Law,* 1850, Translated from the French by Dean Russell, Foreword by Walter E. Williams, Introduction by Richard Ebeling, Afterword by Sheldon Richman, Foundation for Economic Education, 30 South Broadway, Irvington-on-Hudson, NY, 1998. If you only read one book on economic philosophy, make it Frederic Bastiat's *The Law.*

**Chapter 7**

1. John Dalberg-Acton, 1st Baron Acton, Letter to Mandell Creighton (5 April 1887), published in *Historical Essays and Studies, by John*

*Emerich Edward Dalberg-Acton* (1907), edited by John Neville Figgis and Reginald Vere Laurence, Appendix, p. 504; also in *Essays on Freedom and Power*

2. Nancy Pelosi, then Democrat Speaker of the House of Representatives, in a speech before the National Association of Counties annual legislative conference, 9 March 2010
3. Samuel Adams, Boston Gazette 17 Oct. 1768, http://press-pubs.uchicago.edu/founders/documents/amendIIIs2.html
4. Jacob Gershman, Forgotten Third Amendment surfaces in Nevada Case, published on Law Blog, 5 July 2013, http://blogs.wsj.com/law/2013/07/05/forgotten-third-amendment-surfaces-in-nevada-case/ see also Las Vegas Review Journal, "Judge: Police takeover of Henderson Homes not covered by Third Amendment," Carri Geer Thevenot, 16 February 2015, http://www.reviewjournal.com/news/las-vegas/judge-police-takeover-henderson-homes-not-covered-third-amendment and finally "Federal court rejects Third Amendment Claim against police officers," Ilya Somin, The Washington Post online, 23 March 2015 https://www.washingtonpost.com/news/volokh-conspiracy/wp/2015/03/23/federal-court-rejects-third-amendment-claim-against-police-officers/

## Chapter 8

1. James Madison, Federalist #62, Independent Journal, 27 February 1788
2. Josh Withrow, "Key vote no on FY 2016 Omnibus Spending Bill", Freedomworks online, 17 December 2015, http://www.freedomworks.org/content/key-vote-no-fy-2016-omnibus-spending-bill; see also Stephen K. Bannon and Julia Hahn, "Paul Ryan betrays America: $1.1 Trillion, 2000-plus page Omnibus Bill funds "fundamental transformation of America," Breitbart News online, 16 December 2015, http://www.breitbart.com/big-government/2015/12/16/paul-ryan-betrays-america-1-1-trillion-2000-plus-page-omnibus-bill-funds-fundamental-transformation-america/

3. Thomas Jefferson in a letter to John Wayles Eppes, 1813; http://famguardian.org/Subjects/Politics/thomasjefferson/jeff1340.htm

The entire passage in the letter reads as follows:

"We believe--or we act as if we believed--that although an individual father cannot alienate the labor of his son, the aggregate body of fathers may alienate the labor of all their sons, of their posterity, in the aggregate, and oblige them to pay for all the enterprises, just or unjust, profitable or ruinous, into which our vices, our passions or our personal interests may lead us. But I trust that this proposition needs only to be looked at by an American to be seen in its true point of view, and that we shall all consider ourselves unauthorized to saddle posterity with our debts, and morally bound to pay them ourselves; and consequently within what may be deemed the period of a generation, or the life of the majority."
4. U.S. National Debt Clock, The Outstanding Public Debt as of 13 Jan 2016 at 09:26:01 PM GMT; http://www.brillig.com/debt_clock/
5. Benjamin Franklin, , *The Life of Benjamin Franklin, Written by Himself,* edited by John Bigelow, p. 134, Cambridge University Press, first published in 1874
6. W. Cleon Skousen *The 5,000 Year Leap, 28 Great Ideas That Changed the World*, 1979, Copyright 1981, 2009, 5000 Year Leap: 30 Year Anniversary Edition with Glenn Beck Foreword (Kindle Locations 406-415). Packard Technologies. Kindle Edition.
7. James Madison, Federalist 45, *Independent Journal* Saturday, January 26, 1788
8. The United States Conference of Mayors, Impact of Unfunded Federal Mandates and Cost Shifts to US Cities, p. 3, June 2005.
9. Email from Joseph Lightfoot, Chair of the Board of Legislators, St. Lawrence County, NY to author, November 14, 2015

## Chapter 9

1. General Karl von Clausewitz, *On War,* 1873, Translated by Colonel JJ Graham, 1874 was first edition of this translation, 1909 was the

London reprinting; New and Revised edition, with introduction and notes by Colonel F.N. Maude C.B.; release date: 25 February 2006, last updated 26 January 2013; http://www.gutenberg.org/files/1946/1946-h/1946-h.htm

2. Barton Deiters, "Judge orders former pastor arrested for handing out jury nullification pamphlets," Michigan Live online, 1 December 2015, http://www.mlive.com/news/grand-rapids/index.ssf/2015/12/judge_orders_man_arrested_for.html
3. Ibid
4. On Tuesday, February 24th 2014, the Supreme Court ruled that as long as any one person in a home consents, the police have the power to search any private residence, regardless if everyone else at the home refuses. In "Instead of adhering to the warrant requirement," Supreme Court Justice Ginsburg wrote, "today's decision tells the police they may dodge it, nevermind ample time to secure the approval of a neutral magistrate." Tuesday's ruling, she added, "shrinks to petite size our holding in Georgia v. Randolph." The court also ruled that the police can legally search your home without your consent if you're not home. The reasoning is that if you're not home, you can't refuse the search. Matt Agorist, "Supreme Court rules that cops DO NOT need a warrant to search your home," The Free Thought Project.com 25 February, 2014, http://thefreethoughtproject.com/supreme-court-rules-cops-warrant-search-home/#RvZzlTRcxP1mEbUD.99
5. Ronald Reagan: "Inaugural Address," January 20, 1981. Online by Gerhard Peters and John T. Woolley, *The American Presidency Project.* http://www.presidency.ucsb.edu/ws/?pid=43130.

Made in the USA
Middletown, DE
12 March 2016